McCloskey's Rhetoric

The rhetoric of economics has long claimed scientific objectivity; however, the late great economist Joan Robinson argued that "the purpose of studying economics is not to acquire a set of ready-made answers to economic questions, but to learn how to avoid being deceived by economists."

This unique book examines the use of rhetoric in economics, focusing on the work of Deirdre McCloskey as well as other major economic philosophers. Benjamin Balak utilizes the views of Derrida and Foucault amongst others to analyze McCloskey's major texts and critically evaluates the linguistic, literary, and philosophical approaches they introduce.

This book will be of interest to both philosophers and economists alike.

Benjamin Balak is Assistant Professor of Economics at Rollins College, USA.

Routledge INEM advances in economic methodology
Series edited by D. Wade Hands,
Professor of Economics, University of Puget Sound, Tacoma, USA.

The field of economic methodology has expanded rapidly during the last few decades. This expansion has occurred in part because of changes within the discipline of economics, in part because of changes in the prevailing philosophical conception of scientific knowledge, and also because of various transformations within the wider society. Research in economic methodology now reflects not only developments in contemporary economic theory, the history of economic thought, and the philosophy of science; but it also reflects developments in science studies, historical epistemology, and social theorizing more generally. The field of economic methodology still includes the search for rules for the proper conduct of economic science, but it also covers a vast array of other subjects and accommodates a variety of different approaches to those subjects.

The objective of this series is to provide a forum for the publication of significant works in the growing field of economic methodology. Since the series defines methodology quite broadly, it will publish books on a wide range of different methodological subjects. The series is also open to a variety of different types of works: original research monographs, edited collections, as well as republication of significant earlier contributions to the methodological literature. The International Network for Economic Methodology (INEM) is proud to sponsor this important series of contributions to the methodological literature.

1 **Foundations of Economic Method, 2nd Edition**
 A Popperian perspective
 Lawrence A. Boland

2 **Applied Economics and the Critical Realist Critique**
 Edited by Paul Downward

3 **Dewey, Pragmatism and Economic Methodology**
 Edited by Elias L. Khalil

4 **How Economists Model the World into Numbers**
 Marcel Boumans

5 **McCloskey's Rhetoric**
 Discourse ethics in economics
 Benjamin Balak

6 **The Foundations of Paul Samuelson's Revealed Preference Theory**
 A study by the method of rational reconstruction, revised edition
 Stanley Wong

McCloskey's Rhetoric
Discourse ethics in economics

Benjamin Balak

Routledge
Taylor & Francis Group

LONDON AND NEW YORK

First published 2006
by Routledge
2 Park Square, Milton Park, Abingdon, Oxon OX14 4RN

Simultaneously published in the USA and Canada
by Routledge
270 Madison Ave, New York, NY 10016

Routledge is an imprint of the Taylor & Francis Group

© 2006 Benjamin Balak

Typeset in Times New Roman by Wearset Ltd, Boldon, Tyne and Wear
Printed and bound in Great Britain by MPG Books Ltd, Bodmin

British Library Cataloguing in Publication Data
A catalogue record for this book is available from the British Library

Library of Congress Cataloging in Publication Data
A catalog record for this book has been requested

ISBN 0–415–31682–0

To my parents – Naomi and Edo – who taught me the powerful combination of skepticism and ethics, to my family – Charlotte, Félix, and little Thalia – who continue to nurture it, and to my teacher – Vincent Tarascio – who helped me harness it.

Contents

Illustrations

Figure

Tables

1 Exordium

The rhetoric of economics

> The purpose of studying economics is not to acquire a set of ready-made
> answers to economic questions, but to learn how to avoid being deceived
> by economists.
>
> (Joan Robinson, 1955, quoted in Galbraith, 1973)

Over twenty years after the publication of "The Rhetoric of Economics"
in the *Journal of Economic Literature* (1983), Deirdre McCloskey remains
one of the most controversial contemporary economists. In her many texts
following this paper, McCloskey has launched a small but vigorous
community of economists studying the discipline's rhetoric along the lines
suggested by Joan Robinson (see opening quote). While many of her ideas
were borrowed from the humanities, it is in bringing them to bear on the
rhetoric of economics that she has intervened in the history, philosophy,
and methodology of economics. Many in the academic community studying the history of economics have recognized that McCloskey's rhetoric
has had a significant impact on the field and she is mentioned in almost all
texts pertaining in some way to the current understanding of how theories
function in the social sciences (otherwise known as *meta*-theory). Unfortunately, while McCloskey herself is often *mentioned*, very rarely are her
ideas seriously *discussed*. I will argue that the onus is on the majority of
economic philosophers who, to use McCloskey's tongue-in-cheek terminology, *have not done their homework* on recent developments in the philosophy of science, literary and linguistic studies, and that *bête noir*:
epistemology. Once this context is developed, McCloskey's remarkably
accessible prose takes on a host of nuances that most of her highly
sophisticated critics have missed. My first goal is to situate and clarify the
linguistic, literary, and philosophical approaches applied by McCloskey.
Second, to present and criticize the language-theories she adopts, and to
develop several modifications and extensions. Finally, I will attempt to
criticize and evaluate her contributions and their potential consequences
for economics and the social sciences in general.

I proceed with a close reading of some of McCloskey's major texts and the ensuing secondary literature while maintaining my focus on the problem of language. The problem is that language is endogenous to the scientific endeavor at all levels of inquiry. This has been specifically recognized in the 1920s by positivist philosophers of the Vienna Circle, whose initial concerns were with the definition of a scientific *language* that would ensure metaphysics-free positive sciences. The problems they encountered were never resolved in a satisfactory manner due to the analytical feedback created whenever one tries to analyze language. This is because the language under investigation is necessarily contaminated with the language underlying the analysis. Jacques Derrida's deconstruction is particularly useful for studying the structure of language. It provides what could be described as a micro approach for looking at the *processes* of scientific languages in the context of the historical institutions with which they are interdependent. Michel Foucault provides a framework for a macro approach that examines the epistemological history of the social institutions in which knowledge is actually *produced*. Foucault and Derrida have had a tremendous impact on the humanities and the social sciences but their works have scarcely been explicitly introduced and studied within the context of economics (with some rare exceptions in highly specialized contexts). This omission can go some way in explaining the apparent sterility of several recent debates in the sub-fields of economic philosophy and methodology, such as the status and potential of Critical Realism as championed by Tony Lawson's *Economics and Reality* (1997). Much of this important debate is left barren because participants are unaware of the significant work already done on the very same issues by the "continental philosophers." I am convinced that a degree of familiarity with this extensive body of work is necessary in order to overcome several philosophical hurdles that have been arresting the development of the philosophy of economics as well as the historical interpretations of its intellectual history.

Within the texts mentioning, praising, or attacking McCloskey, little is said about the meta-theoretical implications of her work. I will look at the philosophical foundations of the problem of language in science in order to understand the fundamental difficulties that underlie the debate on the rhetorical project in economics. For this purpose, Uskali Mäki's influential critique of McCloskey is particularly helpful (Mäki, 1995). I examine the dialectical relationship between Mäki's analytical reconstruction of McCloskey's epistemological position, and her seemingly incommensurable non-analytical defense. Epistemological issues are behind the intellectual schism between analytical and postmodern philosophy. Using the insights of Derrida, Foucault, and others to adjust scientific epistemology allows me to argue that analytical and postmodern philosophies are not only compatible but also complementary, and probably even interdependent. Furthermore, I argue that only through a thorough understanding of the essential tensions between these two approaches, can one claim to have explained social phenomena to any satisfactory degree of completeness.

Since rhetoric is a thoroughly contextual affair, it is prudent and fruitful to try to retain as much of the text's context as possible. This approach has the advantage of directing the critical focus to the method itself and thus benefits from a continual illustration *by* the text of the points made *in* the text. I work with pairs of texts because the study of interpretation should seek its objects of investigation *within* interpretative relations. These relations are, of course, of different kinds. I will conclude this *exordium* by specifically addressing the three major pairs of texts used:

- McCloskey–Mäki: A seemingly traditional dialectical relation in which Uskali Mäki (critic) rationally reconstructs McCloskey's arguments (primary source) in order to criticize it *externally*: with reference to the logical system of analytical philosophy which is Mäki's but *not* McCloskey's. McCloskey's reply radically departs from the dialectical tradition by rhetorically rejecting it in her *analytically* frivolous response. The rhetoric dissonance created by the *style* of her response foregrounds her *substantial* argument: a deconstruction of the substance/form hierarchical opposition (I'll discuss hierarchical oppositions in detail below). This interpretative relation is rich in incommensurabilities between antagonistic philosophical traditions. This structural antagonism is illuminating in that Mäki's relentless drive to diagnose McCloskey yields a detailed diagram of the points of conflict and the specific rhetoric issues driving them.
- Derrida–Culler: Jacques Derrida's texts are exceedingly difficult to appreciate before embarking on a very long and thorough examination of his own primary sources as well as secondary sources interpreting his almost impenetrable texts. Jonathan Culler is, I believe, the best explicator of Derridian deconstruction. Furthermore, he is surprisingly unknown even though his text *On Deconstruction* (1982) was the only one Derrida himself ever somewhat endorsed. Culler is pedagogically indispensable for his historical narrative, illustrations, and examples. Bringing him to the attention of readers is an objective in itself.
- Foucault–Deleuze: The relationship between Michel Foucault and Gilles Deleuze is more complicated. Both were eminent philosophers who maintained a close personal and professional relationship. Their individual interests led them to apply many of each other's approaches to different domains of philosophy: Foucault operated at the historical, social, and anthropological levels, while Deleuze systematized and applied Foucault's insights at a meta-theoretical level. Such a relationship between the specific and the general will be a major aspect of my analysis. Furthermore, Deleuze is yet to receive the international recognition he deserves as one of the greatest philosophers of the twentieth century.

Following McCloskey's elegant rhetoric example in *Knowledge and Persuasion in Economics* (1994), I structure my text as a classic Greek oration. The *Exordium* (introduction) is followed by a story, the *Narration: McCloskey's Critiques of Economics*, where I reconstruct and interpret McCloskey's criticism of economic methodology and its failure to capture the rhetorical dimension of economic thought. The *Narration* also elaborates on the interdisciplinary elements she introduces into economics and develops them in their disciplinary context. McCloskey's principal antagonist is presented in the *Division: The Mäki diagnosis*. First, Uskali Mäki's careful reconstruction and critique of McCloskey's philosophy is in turn itself reconstructed and then deconstructed. Mäki's work serves to clarify McCloskey's ideas since it rephrases them in a more familiar analytical context. Furthermore, since Mäki's is ostensibly seen as the current philosophical last word on the rhetoric project in economics, he naturally leads to the next section – *Proof: The rhetoric of truth* – discussing the apparent incommensurable aspects of current methodological and philosophical debates in economics. This section includes discussions on the realist-relativist debate, epistemological versus ontological foundations, anti-methodology, and the confusion surrounding postmodernism. In the *Refutation: Beyond ethical neutrality*, I examine the potential use of what has come to be called economic criticism for a thicker understanding of the history of economic thought, as well as the problems and oversights that are raised by such an interdisciplinary approach. I attempt to apply the approaches developed elsewhere in this text to the very issues that are raised by it. In other words, I launch a critique that operates in the same methodological context as its object of investigation and thus functions as an internal criticism at the meta-theoretical level.

Finally, I would like to thank Deirdre McCloskey for discussing many of the issues contained herein with me, the University of North Carolina's Department of Economics, and especially Vincent Tarascio who allowed me to pursue my unorthodox interests unhindered, members of the History of Economics Society and the Eastern Economic Association with whom I discussed many parts of this book, my colleagues at Rollins College who support my research, Rob Langham who is an encouraging and immensely patient editor, and four anonymous referees. I could of course go on to mention many other people without whose direct and indirect help this would never have happened, but will only take this opportunity to apologize for not mentioning them explicitly.

2 Narration

McCloskey's critiques of economics

Exordium: the vices of economics

The principle arguments of McCloskey's rhetoric have been developed in numerous journal articles and books since her pioneering 1983 paper in the *Journal of Economic Literature*. I will focus here primarily on *Knowledge and Persuasion in Economics* (1994) because it reiterates, reinterprets, and develops the principle arguments that appeared in *The Rhetoric of Economics* (1985) and several other texts. *Knowledge and Persuasion* also articulates the philosophical basis of McCloskey's contribution to the discussion on the rhetoric of economics and includes replies to criticism and further refinements and illustrations.

I will attempt to follow a close but concise reading of McCloskey in order to maintain her general structure, which is that of a classical oration. Applying formal Aristotelian structure is such a bombastic appeal to authority that I suspect it is a rhetorical joke. This is a happily common occurrence in McCloskey's prose, and indeed the reason why I chose to imitate this structure in my text. To add my own postmodern twist on the joke, I have nested McCloskey's classically structured argument within the *Narration* of *my* classically structured text. In fact, I hope that this specific *form* is a structural demonstration of the text's *content*. Specifically, I am referring to the inescapable and infinitely regressive relationship between argument and its context.

Jokingly or not, classicism immediately establishes the ideas inhabiting this structure as subscribing to the tenets of the most fundamental orthodoxy of western culture: Aristotelian poetics. The choice employs multiple subtexts and is much more productive than most appeals to authority we regularly use. In both the supposedly distinct realms of the scientific and the rhetoric, Aristotle is more than an authority; he is the paradigm of authority. When McCloskey constantly insists that her rhetoric is *not* radical in any way, who better to legitimize the propriety of her literary tools than Aristotle himself. Finally, there is of course the cultural dimension of introducing continental humanities (i.e. non Anglo) into the Anglo-Saxon halls of science. What better way for a foreign element to disarm xenophobic suspicions, than to pay homage to the local god? In the aforementioned Anglo-Saxon halls of science, that god is still ostensibly a classical Greek.

This structural *apologia* is part of the strategic progression of the text as a whole, which is crafted to allow a gentle entry into the subject, with controversial or difficult issues well prepared so as not to offend an economist's sensibilities. Issues are then revisited later in the text, and only then receive a more careful and consequential analysis.

The immediate issue at hand is then to summarize and evaluate McCloskey's ideas. First, I must decide which of her ideas I will qualify with the adjective *major* and, even harder, which I will not. Having done that I must endeavor to transcribe an idea I have just recognized as *big* into a relatively *small* space without bestowing smallness upon it. I will attempt to escape this burden by letting McCloskey herself do at least part of the job for me: In 1996 she first held the Tinbergen Visiting Professorship at Erasmus University in Rotterdam and presented her ideas in her inaugural address delivered that year. Her *The Vices of Economists – The Virtues of the Bourgeoisie* (1996) is based on this speech and achieves its goal in 130 pages. In it, she argues that the science of economics suffers from three major methodological ills that she refers to as vices: Incorrect and exaggerated use of statistical significance as a means of establishing scientific relevance, increased focus on theoretical modeling at the expense of empirical science, and a continuing belief in social engineering. These three general ideas may seem almost disappointingly banal when appearing in a short list before I present them in an appropriate context. As I will point out on several occasions in this text, McCloskey has a penchant for delivering radical ideas in a seemingly innocent, almost obvious, guise.

The arrogance of social engineering

Let us first dispense with the criticism that McCloskey herself has recently left out of her short-list of complaints. This issue was mute in McCloskey's "Cassandra's Open Letter to her Economist Colleagues" (1999), and since the column claims that the (remaining) two issues have been disregarded by mainstream economics while remaining unsatisfactorily answered, one cannot but speculate as to whether the criticism at hand *has* been heeded, satisfactorily answered, or whether she has simply despaired with getting it across. I'm sorry to say that the latter seems to be the correct observation.

As a historian, McCloskey opens her discussion with a (very) brief survey of the antecedents of the "Tinbergean Vice" which she attributes to the recipient of the first Nobel Memorial Prize in Economic Science – Jan Tinbergen – whose visiting professorship position she was occupying. McCloskey mentions Plato in *The Republic* and August Comte's classical positivism but she does not explicitly address the role of Plato in establishing the disciplinarian urge in western rational thought. A necessary step towards making any sense of these linguistic polemics is to look at the ancient philosophical and historical foundations of the ongoing debate between the philosophers – most notably Plato – and the sophist and rhetoricians. I will return to this below.

The reader may take a detour to *Appendix I: Historical background* for a brief outline of the history of positivism and the growth-of-knowledge sociological traditions that overshadowed it in the second half of the twentieth century.

Comte for his part has the dubious distinction of elaborating his polity in which prediction and power are explicitly linked. His "social physics," developed in his four-volume *System of Positive Polity* (1851–54), still required a *religion* of Humanity to sedate the masses and maintain social order. McCloskey quotes one of his famous slogans: "*prévoir pour pouvoir*," which she translates as "predict in order to control" (McCloskey, 1996: 99) but which I would translate more literally as "predict in order to be capable," which is weaker motivationally but is prior philosophically. Thus before social *control* can be enforced, prediction must *enable* positive statements to escape the limiting space of analytic (logical) statements, in effect invading the no man's land of synthetic (empirical) statements that has been a source of so many difficulties for later positivists. The foundational ritual or magic, which powers Comte's religious system, relies on the act of prediction. Catholics must accept the essential transformability of the body of Christ every Sunday. This involves reiterating the ritual in which his body is transformed into the Eucharist, thus symbolically establishing the possibility of God becoming man and vice versa. This of course opens the way to all sorts of transmogrification in the form of escape from, and thus domination of, what Plato called in the *Symposium* the "mass of perishable rubbish" which is the mortal body. Similarly, the Comtian piteous must accept the potential – and thus symbolic – predictability of nature. The mechanism of predictability is based on the logical symmetry between prediction and explanation: that only an arbitrary temporal difference separates the two. We then have the central positivist idea that successful prediction is tantamount to *true* knowledge in a metaphysical sense. The ground is thus laid for social control and engineering because a social-physicalist (as social engineering was called at the time) agenda is based on an understanding that is in turn justified by prediction. Enlightened Comtians demonstrate their *predictive* magic to a metaphysically driven populous. Social phenomena can thus be *explained* by the same logic that would have predicted them after the fact (*ex post facto*). The very same logic is then applied again in order to devise a social policy that would lead to a different predictable outcome: *prévoir pour pouvoir*.

McCloskey avoids discussing the socio-political relationships between power and knowledge, and this is an important omission in her work. Uskali Mäki raises this issue in his "Diagnosing McCloskey" (1995) by accusing her of being naïve at best and elitist at worst with regard to her social-theory (see *Division* below). McCloskey is content at this stage to characterize control with a quote from Wesley Clair Mitchell:

> [I]n economics as in other sciences we desire knowledge mainly as an instrument of control. Control means the alluring possibility of shaping the evolution of economic life to fit the developing purposes of the race.
>
> (Mitchell, 1924, in McCloskey, 1996: 100)

Putting aside the "erotic fascism" of the above statement, McCloskey addresses the question of what is wrong with attempting to "lay down the future" (McCloskey, 1996: 100). She approaches the task of answering this question from both within and from outside of social engineering itself.

The critique from *within* social engineering is quite trenchant in its simplicity: "Prudent experiment is good" but "profitable prediction is impossible" (McCloskey, 1996: 102). This comes straight out of Fritz Machlup's criticism of Terence Hutchison's positivist economics in their 1950s debates over the pages of the *Southern Economic Journal* (see Caldwell, 1982). McCloskey gives credit to the Austrian economics and Rational Expectations theorists for thoroughly demonstrating the essential impossibility of social engineering by pointing out that it is ourselves that we are trying to engineer. This is the big problem. The reflexivity of economics sets stringent limits on what we can predict and control. "[Social engineering's] ambition to predict and control is bad economics, economics on which every economist agrees" (McCloskey, 1996: 103).

This is not the place for a discussion of the anti-inductivist structural arguments of Austrian economics, the Lucas Critique and other "policy-ineffectiveness" arguments, or the Theorem of Modest Greed, which could probably be seen as central to modern macroeconomic curricula. I will spare non-economist readers and explain them only when absolutely necessary. To this illustrious list, McCloskey adds what she calls The American Question: "If he's so smart, why isn't he rich?" (McCloskey, 1996: 103). The wide acceptance of these criticisms may explain why the issue of social engineering has become less pertinent to McCloskey. After all, Chicago School economics with its sophisticated advocacy of laissez faire is hardly heterodox at the turn of *this* century. This would however be far too simple an explanation because while Chicago economics is indeed highly influential academically, it quickly becomes entangled in political-economic interests when applied to actual policy decisions. The nuances of the analysis end up having little influence at the political level except for as a metaphysical rhetorical ritual in which homage is paid to the gods of competition (à la Comte) while regulations (or lack thereof) continue serving powerful monopolies.

The external criticism of social engineering is that it is "hostile to freedom" (McCloskey, 1996: 115). Here, too, McCloskey forwards an historical argument according to which economics combines the two central socio-political ideas of the Enlightenment: liberal freedom and social rationality. The former is embodied in the works of John Stuart Mill and the latter in those of Jeremy Bentham. Economics' great synthesis, according to McCloskey and the Chicago School, would thus be between these two ideas in the form of the "doctrine that leaving people alone is the most rational policy, and will result in the greatest utility. Voila! Being free results in the most rationality" (McCloskey, 1996: 117). McCloskey however recognizes that this doctrine is far from universally applicable and that a utilitarian rational utopia may be, and often is, incompatible with individual liberties, just as a libertarian utopia may fail to maximize social utility.

The futility of blackboard economics

This vice is named after Paul Samuelson and is characterized initially as the common yet irritating complaint in which academics are often accused of "staying always in a world of theory, spending an academic career imagining alternative worlds in which the sea is boiling hot and pigs have wings" (McCloskey, 1996: 64). Samuelson is obviously not alone and is singled out for his unequaled influence on modern economics. As an example, McCloskey sites Samuelson's 1940s proof that it is only in the absence of externalities that markets can give rise to social optima. Externalities are more commonly known as spillover effects: Costs and benefits that affect parties not directly involved in an exchange (for example, pollution, education, policing, military, etc.) When an economic agent is obliged to sustain a loss or incur a cost without compensation, there can be no presumption that both parties to the exchange are made better off. Consequently, government intervention may lead to a better social outcome. This proof was used to champion government intervention in diverse areas of public and private life, from protecting the environment to the war on drugs. There is however a crucial missing element: Externalities may very well be a *necessary* condition to justify government intervention in markets, but it certainly is not a *sufficient* condition. This is because if one considers that (i) the question of how big must spillover effects be in order to justify intervention is left entirely unanswered, and (ii) the caveats of social engineering (see previous section) lead one to suspect that the outcome of intervention may not prove better, and perhaps may even be worse than in the case of non-intervention. Samuelson's proof raises interesting questions about the relative effectiveness of markets under different conditions, but it also provides an open-ended and empirically empty tool for political coercion. It is empirically empty because it merely states the *existence of the possibility* of a better outcome brought about by government intervention. It does not suggest anything about the effects of government regulation or the sort of regulation that may be useful under different conditions. It is open-ended because it does not even conceptually attempt to *measure* the effects of an externality and thus *any* degree of external effects associated with *any* exchange justifies *any* extent of government regulation. This is of course in effect a carte blanche for the erosion of any and all civil liberties since, to some extent, all exchange affects individuals external to that particular exchange. Used in this way, Samuelson's theoretical analysis of the functioning of markets when there are spillover effects becomes a tool for those who interpret democracy as a dictatorship of the majority.

It is important to note that McCloskey is not at all opposed to the use of mathematics in economics. She takes issue with the appropriation by economics of the wrong scientific *values*: mathematics and logic instead of the natural sciences. According to McCloskey, the values of mathematics and formal logic are consistency, rigor, and conclusions that follow axioms. The oppositions on which these values rest are summarized in Table 1.

If mathematical economists would take the time to familiarize themselves with the work of their colleagues in the natural science departments, they would have to concur with the observations of the mathematical economist William Brock:

> When studying the natural science literature in this area it is important for the economics reader, especially the economic theorist brought up on the tradition of abstract general equilibrium theory, to realize that many natural scientists are not impressed by mathematical arguments showing that "anything can happen" in a system loosely disciplined by general axioms. Just showing the existence of logical possibilities is not enough for such skeptics. The parameters of the system needed to get the erratic behavior must conform to parameter values established by empirical studies or behavior must be actually documented in nature.
>
> (Brock, 1988: 2, in McCloskey, 1996: 82–3)

McCloskey does not deny the crucial usefulness of mathematical tools in the development of economic models but rather bemoans the lack of scientific values to direct them. A rather shocking example is the story she tells of a committee of the American Economic Association that was set

Table 1 The ethos (character, values) of the math department

Mathematical values	Scientific values
Timeless and exact proof	Approximations
Axiomatization	Experience
Qualitative truths	Quantitative truths
Existence	Magnitude

up to discuss the results of a study conducted by Arjo Klamer and David Collander in 1990. Graduate students in leading economics departments in the United States were asked whether it was desirable for an economist's career to have a "thorough knowledge of the economy." Only 3 percent of the respondents selected "very important" while 68 percent considered such knowledge as "unimportant." "Being interested in, and good at, empirical research" was deemed "unimportant" by 23 percent of the sample, but "excellence in mathematics" was rated as "very important" by 57 percent of the sample (Klamer and Colander, 1990: 18). Having completed my graduate studies in a leading economics department during the 1990s, I am quite familiar with this macho student ethos.

The crux of the matter is in the confusion between *truth* and *validity*. The latter is a philosophical term specifically referring to the consistent and rigorous logical progression from an assumption A to a conclusion C. McCloskey presents what she whimsically calls "the proof against proofs" to illustrate the principle that "one can always devise a set of logical connections to get conclusions C from assumptions A as long as one is free to choose A" (McCloskey, 1996: 83). The whimsicality of her proof is actually a deconstruction of the logic of existence theorems in which the very existence of the scientific relevance of existence theorems in economics is questioned on its own terms. At the same time this metatheorem (a theorem about theorems) goes beyond the commonsense point that an assumption A can always be found from which conclusion C can rigorously be derived. The small but important addition is that the problem of magnitudes is addressed. Specifically, the idea that an assumption A′ that is arbitrarily *close* to assumption A can imply a conclusion C′ that is arbitrarily *far* from conclusion C. In other words, even small changes in assumptions can lead to very big changes in conclusions, thus rendering theory useless for economic policy in an approximate world.

In *Knowledge and Persuasion in Economics* (1994: 148), McCloskey defines formalism in economics as subscribing to "the Claim" that knowledge in the form of a system of existence theorems is the *only* true economic knowledge. She uses general equilibrium theory as an example: Formalist economists (Arrow–Debreu and Arrow–Hahn) have constructed theorems that give some necessary and sufficient conditions for exact efficiency but do not engage in the *economically necessary* policy issue of how closely these conditions need to be satisfied to yield *approximate* efficiency. Internal attacks on such work primarily focus on how adding a few assumptions or removing "unreasonable" others could undermine the efficiency – opposite point of view, same rhetoric.

McCloskey finds a surprising ally in the mathematical microeconomist Hal Varian, who published a paper on the subject with the philosopher Allan Gibbard in the *Journal of Philosophy* (1979). They describe how a McCloskean quantitative rhetoric of approximation would be incorporated into a mathematical economic model but concede that this rhetoric is almost always left unspecified and thus impotent in relating the black-board world to the real world.

> When a model is applied to a situation as an approximation of the conclusions … If the assumptions of the applied model were true to a degree of approximation delta, its conclusions would be true to a degree epsilon … of course … few if any of the degrees of approximation involved are characterized numerically.
>
> (Gibbard and Varian, 1979: 671–2)

Varian and Gibbard are explicitly transcribing the problem of magnitudes – how big is big – into their deductive model as parameters, but shirk from the task of evaluating the values of these parameters by empirical studies or any other method; not even an educated guess.

McCloskey produces an amusing irony that hides an important key to understanding how she fits into the history of the philosophy of science. She refers to her metatheorem according to which any given assumption A' that is arbitrarily close to assumption A, can imply a conclusion C' that is arbitrarily far from conclusion C. She then states that unlike most economic theorists she can actually use her metatheorem to predict behavior!

> Take any recent "finding" from the blackboard. I predict that if the "finding" is thought to be important enough then within a short time there will appear a paper by Economist Number Two showing that by making an alternative assumption A' the "finding" is reversed. And shortly afterwards a paper will appear (written perhaps by the thesis student of Economist Number One) in which a set of assumptions A" will reinstate the old conclusion. And so forth. I predict further that the steam will eventually run out of the "research program," when it starts to dawn on people that nothing has been proven one way or the other by this latest "work" on the blackboard. Economists will simply drop the so-called "findings." Then a great genius will appear, who will produce a different "finding," and the story will start all over again. It's not science.
>
> (McCloskey, 1996: 89)

Like a Shakespearean fool, McCloskey offers the economist-reader a caricature of herself. She is often accused of employing the commonplace dialectic strategy of erecting a straw-man reconstruction of one's opponent, and then joyfully setting it aflame. My reading of this caricature shows that this is hardly the case here. She is presenting a short, descriptive growth-of-knowledge model in the Kuhnian or even Lakatosian tradition. Before continuing, I will very briefly present these theories and direct the reader to Caldwell (1982) and many other sources for a more adequate description.

The most famous philosopher of science is Thomas Kuhn, whose *The Structure of Scientific Revolutions* (1962) has become iconic of the contemporary rise of skepticism in the philosophy and methodology of science. The basis of his theory is the distinction between "normal science" and "revolutionary science," and the concepts according to which the distinction is made: paradigm and paradigm-shift. Normal science is a science that follows the example of previous science and follows the prescriptive framework delineated by the paradigm to which it belongs. Normal science specifically does not problematize aspects of the paradigm and seeks only to extend the received view and, more importantly, perform the pedagogical function of training new scientists in the specific paradigm-lore.

Imre Lakatos (1970a and b) could be seen as representing the "state-of-the-art" paradigm for strongly prescriptive methodology in the philosophy of science. The central feature of "sophisticated methodological falsificationism" is its evolutionary view of research traditions as constituted from a dynamic series of theories, which evolve through time and compete with each other over which series is better able to adapt to falsifying evidence that emerges in a fluid scientific environment. These adaptations are accomplished with "problemshifts" which can be seen as mutations in the series of theories that constitute a research program. The implicit evolutionary description of science – though rhetorically convincing – relies on heuristic principles with doubtful descriptive power. Caldwell (1982) has argued that Lakatos's most important divergence from his mentor Sir Karl Popper is that he de-emphasizes refutation by decisive tests and relies entirely on adjudging problemshifts for their progressiveness: the ability to anticipate new facts (theoretically progressive) of which some are corroborated (empirically progressive). This implies that falsification does not necessarily lead to a rejection of a theory unless a ready alternative is available. Lakatos introduced heuristic strategies designed to police the balance of continuity and progress in research programs. This balance is maintained with a "refutable protective belt" within which progressive problemshifts are allowed to carry new information to the refutable variants of the research program, while the irrefutable "hard-core" safeguards the continuity of the program.

In a Lakatosian research program the irrefutable hard-core is protected from even progressive problemshifts by an absolute negative heuristics tied to the entire set of ideas forming the hard-core. In Kuhn's view, there is an *endogenous* mechanism by which the paradigm is protected. I would call it "indoctrination-by-doing," a variant of the familiar economic concept of learning-by-doing that is a part of production theory, and refers to the phenomena by which human capital (workers' skills) and thus productivity rise with experience. Kuhn, like Lakatos, believed continuity to be paramount and considered this aspect of normal science as beneficial. By founding his paradigms on the concept of socialization, Kuhn significantly softens the

Lakatosian hard-core while specifying an underlying mechanism that can be observed and studied.

For Kuhn, a new idea emerges from normal science through a process of accumulating anomalies. The pedantic drive of normal science inevitably discovers and exposes problems and contradictions in the paradigm which, having reached a certain critical mass, result in crisis. If practitioners are unable to reconcile the anomalies with the existing paradigm then a revolution ensues in which a new paradigm challenges the incumbent. The point made in the last sentence is that the symptoms of crisis are in fact attempts at constructing and establishing a new paradigm *not* in order to eliminate normal science but in order to enable normal science to proceed again. The revolutionary prerequisite of an alternative paradigm has two important consequences that challenge both falsificationism and empiricism in general, and the very idea of a single prescriptive methodology. First, theories are accepted or rejected based not only on inconsistencies with data, but also on a comparison with *other theories* and their structural position within their paradigm. Second, Kuhn specifically asserts that with a change in paradigm come not only changes in predictions, descriptions, and explanations but also changes in method and domain, which are the basis of the positivist distinction between scientific (enlightened) and metaphysical (superstitious) knowledge. "The normal-scientific tradition that emerges from a scientific revolution is not only incompatible but often actually incommensurable with that which has gone before" (Kuhn, 1970: 103). Herein lay the seeds of the social-constructivist paradigm in contemporary philosophy of science. If standards and criteria for theory choice are contextually tied to a specific paradigm, a scientific revolution renders these standards obsolete. It follows therefore that there is no single methodology that will ensure progress towards the truth no matter how broadly the latter is defined.

A Kuhnian reading of McCloskey's caricature would yield a world in which a paradigm gains acceptance by virtue of its outstanding mathematical and logical *form* – the elegance with which it is presented rigorously and without contradiction as a set of assumptions deductively leading to a set of conclusions. Normal science then proceeds to produce innumerable series of A', A'', A''' ... and corresponding C', C'', C''' ... in which no reference is made to any parameters of an external or real world and thus any adjustments that are made are exercises or variations on the original composition. My vocabulary is drifting inescapably to musical terminology since the picture emerging from the Kuhnian analysis suggests that modern formalist economics resembles the formal structures of Baroque music. Kuhn sees normal science as his engine of progress because it is through its incessant reapplication and re-testing that anomalies are accumulated, and are either incorporated into the paradigm or, if they are incompatible, scientific revolutions occur and new paradigms arise to set an example for the normal science to come. In McCloskey's caricature, normal science is an exercise in which different deductive structures are applied to an arbitrary theoretical world like different literary styles and devices are applied to the same arbitrary skeletal story in the literary form known as an *exercices de style* (see Raymond Queneau, 1947). Unlike in physics, an anomaly need not be *explained* in order for the paradigm to succeed. The anomaly merely needs to be *corrected* since it is merely a *logical* mistake. *Mathematical formalism in economics is thus portrayed as having disabled the revolutionary potential of Kuhnian normal science – the very mechanism driving scientific innovation and progress.* The void is filled by the chillingly pathetic observation that what finally brings about a new paradigm is the practitioners' eventual boredom and desire for a new style to work in.

McCloskey describes a process in the evolution of a research program, a term she uses to evoke Imre Lakatos's "sophisticated methodological falsificationism." This is hardly a straw-man and is arguably the most robust articulation of positivist scientific methodology. The Lakatosian research program is a structure of heuristic strategies designed to "police" the balance of continuity and progress in a series of theories in which "each subsequent theory results from adding auxiliary clauses to (or from semantically reinterpreting of) the previous theory in order to accommodate some anomaly" (Lakatos, 1970b). To be progressive and allowed into the program's corpus, each new theory in a series of theories must have some corroborated excess empirical content over its predecessor. Each new theory must thus lead us to the actual discovery of some new fact. The negative heuristics block access to the *conventionally established* irrefutable core of the research program. The negative heuristic assures continuity and is relatively unproblematic: it defends the collection of assumptions, methods, and ideologies that make one research program distinctive from another – its values and character (ethos).

In McCloskey's caricature however the negative heuristic *is* problematic because the irrefutable hard-core of Samuelsonian economics consists of an aesthetic adherence to mathematical formalism. This implies a blurred distinction between logical *validity* and scientific *truth*. Continuity is Lakatos's fundamental link to reality. This realism in his work can be seen as a generally progressive movement towards an absolute truth without actually ever attaining *The* Truth. This view – fallibilism is the term coined by Alfred Tarski (1956) – still allows for the existence of criteria that may allow us to occasionally recognize error. In my view, Lakatos's most brilliant move is to harnesses this epistemological link more successfully than his mentor Karl Popper. The existence of the mere *possibility* of recognizing error – even if highly unlikely – is enough to reinstate reality. If progressive series of theories can be made to steer away from error on those occasions when error can be ascertained, then given enough time, we can say that we have made some progress in the general direction of The Truth. This is the mechanism in a Lakatosian research program that establishes a realistic justification for science as a progression towards truth (albeit a chaotic random walk). Economists who are supposedly subscribed to this ideal cannot seriously hold that they are approximating it if they never confront their ideas with the world. If the positive heuristic is nothing but logical validity then Bertrand Russell and Alfred Whitehead's *Principia Mathematica* (1910–13) was in fact the illusive *philosopher's stone*, and science has since closed shop. Any idea presented rigorously and without contradiction as a set of assumptions deductively leading to a set of conclusions is valid. No novel facts or predictions are necessary, and the delicate balance between continuity and innovation is abandoned. My reading of McCloskey's caricature highlights how mathematical formalism is detrimental to the scientific progress of economics according to its *own* methodological criteria; hence an *internal* critique.

McCloskey does not rely on the reader to embark on these philosophical readings of her little joke. She chooses instead to make sure her point is understood by arguing that the same criticism that is increasingly accepted in relation to general equilibrium models is just as applicable to the more fashionable corpus of game theory. McCloskey presents a typical game-theoretical situation in which a utility-maximizing agent (Max U) finds himself in a non-cooperative Nash equilibrium better known as the Prisoner's Dilemma. She reads this scenario as a restatement of Thomas Hobbes's problem in which he asks: "Will a group of unsocialized brutes form spontaneously a civil society?"

> Again and again economists have said, pointing to the blackboard, "No: unsocialized brutes like Max U will defect from social arrangements. Boy is that *interesting!*" That might be silly to spend three centuries trying to solve a problem positing such a strange A – that people are *not* already French or gendered or raised in families or in other ways socialized to an array of vices and virtues – has not occurred to the men of economics.
>
> (McCloskey 1996: 95)

McCloskey does allow that some "men of economics" have been aware of the social phenomenon of cooperation. She gives nodding mention to experimental economics and the "new" economic history, and recognizes that game theorists themselves have accepted that "people do cooperate; finite prisoner's dilemma games unravel, making cooperation inexplicable; but infinite games, as the Folk Theorem says, have an infinite number of solutions" (ibid.). Since an infinite number of solutions are useless for science, game theorists should address this major weakness of the hardcore of their paradigm instead of, or at least before, embarking on a realistically unbounded exploration of the associated "hyperspace of assumptions" (McCloskey, 1994: 137, 141–3, 168, and 172–3). It is nonsensical to study *social*-strategy in a theoretical world from which the relevant social-phenomena – most obviously cooperation and its institutions of family, trust, or charity for example – have been artificially removed. McCloskey neglects to mention Vilfredo Pareto's *Trattato di sociologia generale* (1916, translated to English as *The Mind and Society*, 1932) in which he anticipates some of the modern concerns with atomistic economic agents. Vincent Tarascio (1968, 1969, and 1974) discusses Pareto's utility theory in which he explicitly models what has come to be known as intersubjectivity. In his formulation, each individual's utility function includes other individuals' weighted utilities. Applying this framework is still even conceptually overwhelming but there may be some hope if economists develop increasingly sophisticated simulations running on increasingly powerful computers.

The irrelevance of statistical significance

I have left for last the Kleinian vice, named after Lawrence R. Klein whose *A Textbook of Econometrics* (1953) can be seen as the *urtext* (an original text or earliest version) of regression analysis in economics. It seems to me that this third complaint is probably the most urgent for McCloskey. It is in this aspect of economics that she has seen fit to "leak" to the lay public in two articles in *Scientific American* (1995b, 1995c), and to discuss in her "Cassandra's Open Letter to her Economist Colleagues" (1999: 361). Her enthusiasm is most probably driven by the explicit and implicit recognition of her criticism among econometricians. She has thus chosen to focus on this vice more often than on the others simply because she has made some headway and hopes to make a significant dent in this highly detrimental process of economics.

This criticism is closely related to the Samuelsonian vice (the futility of blackboard economics) in that both are to be remedied with a prescription of a quantitative rhetoric. This similarity is initially surprising since the Samuelsonian vice is essentially an escapist taste for formal *deduction* while the Kleinian Vice seems to concern overconfidence in *inductive* methods. Indeed while the quantitative rhetoric missing from the Samuelsonian vice is that of approximation, the quantitative rhetoric missing in the Kleinian vice addresses a question of quantitative balance. A scientifically significant empirical study of the tradeoff between unemployment and the minimum wage, for example, must address two facts: Higher wages will benefit employees who remain employed, while, at the same time, employers will hire less labor and thus some of the previously employed (albeit at sub-minimum wage) will lose their jobs. These two facts operate as two poles between which some balance has to be struck. Declaring that the tradeoff *exists* based on some sort of statistical corroboration is a step in the right direction from merely deducing that under assumptions A, tradeoff C may *exist*. However, it still does not produce a viable basis for employment policy because it fails to explicitly address the *human* question of balance.

In other words, how big a diversion from the balance is to be considered a significantly big imbalance? If we estimate that increasing the minimum wage by 50 cents would raise unemployment by 1 percent, what is the societal impact? How many people are better or worse off? How much better or worse off are they? Only by addressing these questions can an empirical study serve as a justifiable basis for policy.

> The tragedy came, as tragedies sometimes do, in a tiny detail of the story. Or at any rate it looks at first like a tiny detail, such as the tiny detail of King Oedipus's fight with an older man on a lonely highway or the tiny detail of the exact form of King Lear's will and testament to his three daughters. The detail is the phrase that goes along with regression, "statistical significance."
>
> (McCloskey, 1996: 27)

Like Oedipus and Lear, many economists are unaware of the consequences of the little detail behind the tragedy. In "The Standard Error of Regression," McCloskey and Stephen Ziliak (1996) find that 96 percent of empirical papers published in the 1980s in the *American Economic Review* misused statistical significance. Worse yet, 70 percent offered policy proposals based solely on misused t-statistics (the basis of statistical significance). That is a lot of economic tragedy. Furthermore, economic tragedy inevitably leads to human tragedy because, as John Maynard Keynes famously remarked:

> The ideas of economists and political philosophers, both when they are right and when they are wrong, are more powerful than is commonly understood. Indeed the world is ruled by little else. Practical men, who believe themselves to be quite exempt from any intellectual influences, are usually the slaves of some defunct economist.
>
> (Keynes, 1936: 383)

Before discussing exactly what is economically wrong with using statistical significance in lieu of scientific significance I would like to raise some relevant methodological issues. Taking *results* from a statistical regression and then interpreting their scientific importance based on how well the regression *itself* performed is a methodological tautology. Empirical tools do not generate conclusions, but results that require interpretation. The econometrician may choose to stop here after having taken economic raw material and refined it to a degree. Somebody however must engage in scientific inquiry for the observations to be of scientific value. A scientist must construct some sort of explanatory *conclusion*. Conclusion is a purely human concept that does not exist in nature. We need it to draw policy proposals, and if conclusion is defined sufficiently broadly as a degree of rational closure, then we need it to be able to conceptualize the world. This closure cannot be attained from the numbers alone, just as much as a traveler cannot ascertain his whereabouts by looking at his vehicle's fuel efficiency.

McCloskey quotes Klein's use of the by now formulaic following rhetoric in his first scientific paper, published in 1943:

> The role of Y in the regression is not statistically significant. The ratio of the regression coefficient to its standard error is only 1.812 [this is the t-statistic]. This low value of the ratio means that we *cannot* reject the hypothesis that the true value of the regression coefficient is zero.
>
> (Klein, 1985, in McCloskey, 1996: 31)

As Klein's new method increasingly gained popularity as the harbinger of a hitherto unattained degree of positive knowledge, advances in computing power allowed the creation of an econometric cottage industry which has since transformed into "Satanic Mills," to use William Wordsworth's poetic description of nineteenth century British industry.

McCloskey's argument against the misuse of statistical significance in economics rests on the claim that a variable's statistical significance has little bearing on the *scientific* question of which variables are *economically* important in understanding and explaining phenomena. This leads to a methodologically significant internal criticism: Dropping a scientifically significant variable because it is statistically insignificant could very well invalidate all subsequent work since the results would become, to use econometric jargon, biased and inconsistent.

> It is simply not the case that statistically insignificant coefficients are in effect zero. The experiments on aspirin and heart disease were halted short of statistical significance (at the level the medical researchers wanted to have) because the effect was so large in life-saving terms that it was immoral to go on with the double-blind experiment in which some people did not get their daily dose of aspirin.
>
> (McCloskey, 1996: 35)

In McCloskey's example, scientists decided that a certain number of deaths were a *morally* sufficient magnitude to warrant the conclusion that aspirin had a *medically* significant effect on heart disease. This was done despite the fact that by stopping the experiment short they were forced to accept a degree of fuzziness in the estimate – measured by statistical significance – lower than they previously had hoped to attain. To paraphrase Klein's 1943 jargon-setting paper (see original quote from Klein above): *The role of the dummy-variable ASPIRIN in the regression is not statistically significant. The ratio of the regression coefficient to its standard error is very low which means that we cannot reject the hypothesis that the true value of the regression coefficient is zero.* Thankfully, the medical researchers could and did reject the hypothesis that aspirin has no effect on heart disease.

Econometricians however are not as foolish as they may seem in this section. Many of the issues raised here and others raised elsewhere have been and are being addressed. Most importantly, econometricians are increasingly adopting methods *and* values from the engineering and physics departments. Specifically, the same increase in computing power that may have led to the obsessive and erroneous use of regression analysis may now have gotten to the point that simulations are becoming practical in economics. If indeed there is – as many econometricians are quick to claim – ready econometric solutions to McCloskey's problems, then perhaps the following passage may be overly bleak:

> The situation is like the proverbial joke about the drunk discovered by his friend crawling around close to a lamppost on a dark night. "What are you doing?" "I'm looking for my keys. I dropped them." "Oh, I'll help you. Did you drop them here?" "No, I dropped them over there in the dark ... But the light's better here." Statistical economists since they began to indulge in the Kleinian vice have been drunks searching for economic truth under a lamppost, instead of out in the dark where it is to be found. Looking in the dark is more difficult, admittedly. But that's not an argument for staying under the lamppost. That science is difficult and pseudo-science is easy is not an argument for adopting pseudo-science.
>
> (McCloskey, 1996: 33)

The virtues of the bourgeoisie

I have been discussing the three vices McCloskey accuses modern economics of indulging in without any mention of the bourgeois virtues that she is apparently advocating. The only candidate for virtue so far is what she calls the *values of science*: useful and applicable explanation, as opposed to the values of mathematics and formal logic: formulaic elegance. She acknowledges that accepting the vices as such does not readily suggest what economists should be doing instead. This criticism has often been raised against what I would very broadly call the Crisis in Economics literature. These critics of economics are accused of continuously and *mechanistically* repeating a set of by now well-worn problematic issues. The degree to which these issues are seen as critical varies but there is one question that continues to hang over the heads of these critics like the Sword of Damocles. This is the same question McCloskey asks of axiomatic or Samuelsonian economists: "*So What?* What have you taught me about the actual economic world? Not hypothetical worlds, but the one we live in. And how do you know?" (McCloskey, 1996: 124). I will attempt to answer this question in detail and at different levels of inquiry including the meta-theoretical in my text. At this point however I will address it at the levels I have primarily employed in *this* section: McCloskey's descriptions and, when available, prescriptions regarding how economists explain the economy. This is the traditional domain of methodology.

McCloskey's prescription against social engineering is as straightforward as her criticism: Erect or facilitate the erection of institutions that should change the economy in a beneficial way while making all possible efforts to design them to be non-damaging. What emerges as her main concern however is the *culture* of the economics community: The academic institutions that govern the selection and indoctrination of economics graduate students, and the institutions that archive and ossify the values that they learn (peer-reviewed journals for example). The 97 percent of graduate students in leading departments who did *not* consider having knowledge of the economy as very important, have been groomed, or, more descriptively, *brutalized* into adhering so religiously to what McCloskey calls the values of the math department. This concern – though quite real – is a very general concern with the institutions of academia. In Lakatosian terms, it could be restated as a misbalance between continuity and progress in the economics research program. Too much is left unquestioned in the irrefutable hard-core while the positive heuristic mediating the refutable protective belt is based on formalistic and esthetically determined criteria. McCloskey urges us to incessantly remind "the A-Primers, who are often in a minority, though an arrogant and intolerant one" (McCloskey, 1996: 124), that their dogma fails to satisfy its own stated criteria of what is a science. McCloskey is employing the good old positivist criteria of cognitive significance against those who would claim to be its guardians: Too much of economics is metaphysical. It is perhaps surprising to associate McCloskey with positivist methodology. Nevertheless, I find that her criticism of the Samuelsonian vice echoes much of the logical positivists' discussion of the status of theories in science during the 1920s and 1930s.

In many instances, McCloskey reiterates her allegiance to the Chicago School of economics. As a Chicago economist, she believes that the rotten equilibrium in which modern economics finds itself is not sustainable. Nevertheless, like any reasonable (dare I say sophisticated) non-interventionist, she believes that the invisible hand could use gentle guidance. She proposes her *ethics* for this purpose and suggests that an ethical change is necessary inside economics:

> Economists have believed for about a century that they are *wertfrei*, practitioners of the positive rather than the normative. I believed this once myself. It is wrong. I report what I have heard from friends on the frontier of science studies, sociologists and philosophers and historians of science. They have concluded that scientists are not the romantic yet objective, passionate yet masculine heroes they would like to be considered, and which the philosopher Karl Popper made them out to be.

Scientists are *actual people*. This startling assertion from science studies over the past quarter century means that science, like the rest of life, is an ethical matter ... I take "ethos" in its Greek meaning as "character," the character we live moment by moment in the home or the laboratory or the library. Ethics in science is rarely about spectacular cases of lying. It is about the ethical character from which the scientist acts in judging a coefficient on the minimum wage large.

(McCloskey, 1996: 125–6)

This is not the place to argue over McCloskey's characterization of Popper but I cannot restrain myself from saying that while I could definitely accept romantic, passionate, and masculine, Popper's view of scientists can perhaps be characterized as idealistic for his insistence that scientists are honest in *seeking* objectivity, but he never believed that they are *actually* objective.

By basing her ethics on a restatement of the Marxian theory of ideology and the ensuing problems with the possibility of *ethical neutrality*, McCloskey sets a deterministic tone for her historical reading of the modernist ethos in economics. What is the modernist ethos? *The Electronic Labyrinth* at the University of Virginia has a particularly useful schema:

1. premodernism: Original meaning is possessed by authority (for example, the Catholic Church). The individual is dominated by tradition.
2. modernism: The enlightenment-humanist rejection of tradition and authority in favour of reason and natural science. This is founded upon the assumption of the autonomous individual as the sole source of meaning and truth – the Cartesian cogito. Progress and novelty are valorized within a linear conception of history – a history of a "real" world that becomes increasingly real or objectified. One could view this as a Protestant mode of consciousness.
3. postmodernism: A rejection of the sovereign autonomous individual with an emphasis upon anarchic collective, anonymous experience. Collage, diversity, the mystically unrepresentable, Dionysian passion are the foci of attention. Most importantly, we see the dissolution of distinctions, the merging of subject and object, self and other. This is a sarcastic playful parody of western modernity and the "John Wayne" individual and a radical, anarchist rejection of all attempts to define, reify or re-present the human subject.

(Morley, 1993: n.p.)

In this context, the three vices of economics can be seen as sub-vices to the arch-vice of pride. This vice is explained in an intriguing variation on class struggle: Modernism (and modern economics) has a bipolar rhetoric of virtue. On the one hand are the *pagan* virtues of courage, justice, temperance, and prudence that characterize a hero in the classical sense. Different heroes have different mixes of these virtues – consider the differences between Achilles and Odysseus – but can be associated with an *aristocratic* ethos. On the other hand are the *monotheistic* virtues of faith, hope, and love that characterize a saint, and can be associated with a *peasant* ethos. "But we are neither heroes nor saints. We are bourgeois, town dwellers. Yet we do not have a vocabulary of bourgeois virtue" (McCloskey, 1996: 126).

McCloskey evokes classical liberalism and especially the Scottish Enlightenment of David Hume and Adam Smith as an example modern economics should follow. However, her use of Adam Smith to show how his economic ethos was not only based on the prudence of *The Wealth of Nations* (Smith, 1799) but also on the temperance of *The Theory of Moral Sentiments* (1801) and the justice of his *Lectures on Jurisprudence* (1978) is confusing. This is because she seems to be attributing the aristocratic virtues to Smith while, at the same time, presenting him as an example of bourgeois virtues. A malicious reader could attribute this to a moralistic twist on the bourgeoisie's envy of the aristocracy. The class-metaphor picks up the story after the bourgeoisie overtook the aristocracy as the dominant class in society. By the turn of the last century however,

> the intelligentsia became increasingly alienated from the bourgeois world from which it sprung, and wished to become something Higher. It wished to make novels difficult and technical – think of Woolf or Joyce – to keep them out of the hands of the uneducated and to elevate the intelligentsia to a new clerisy, a new aristocracy of the spirit.
>
> (McCloskey, 1996: 127)

The arch-vice of pride within which all three vices of economics are contained turns out to be the social aspirations of the nouveaux riches. McCloskey's little story tells us something about the social psychology behind the arrogance of modernism but only vaguely sketches the bourgeois economics that she advocates. She has since been working on an exhaustive four-volume project under the working title of *The Bourgeois Virtues: Ethics for an Age of Capitalism*, which I will return to at the end of this text.

A much clearer picture can be found in the last pages of *The Vices of Economists – The Virtues of the Bourgeoisie* (1996) where she employs a metaphor linking the workings of the markets for goods and services and the workings of economics. This link will also lead to the following section where I will endeavor to produce a more extensive critique of McCloskey's rhetoric and her language and discourse-theories.

The way good science works is the way a good market works, not
anonymously and mechanically as we economists so often think, but
through trust, conversation, persuasion. Arjo Klamer and I have discovered that one-quarter of the national income is spent on persuasion, sweet talk. A bourgeois society depends on lengthy discussions
of what to do.

...

As our century of the European nightmare ends, a nightmare formed
from the aristocratic and peasant dreams of the 19th century, we need
to honor a new set of virtues, suiting the marketplace as much as the
academy. It is no linguistic accident that the word *forum*, which means
with us "place of open discussion," started its life meaning "marketplace," a place of bourgeois virtue. It is no accident, either, that the
agora of Greece was where Greek democracy happened.

(McCloskey, 1996: 128, 130)

Not surprisingly, McCloskey's methodological critique of economics is
inseparable from her philosophy of economics as much as it is inseparable from her politics. McCloskey's overriding prescription in which all
others are contained is the call for *sprachethik*: an ethos of conversation.
The concept is borrowed from Jorgen Habermas and is usually translated as discourse-ethic. It proves to be very problematic on several
levels and will be addressed at length below. First, I must turn to
McCloskey's conversational ethos as it is employed in her philosophical
arguments.

Narration: the conversation of economics

The initial question McCloskey raises in *Knowledge and Persuasion*
regards how intellectual fads move among disciplines. She gives numerous
examples, most of which deal with the increasing use of mathematics in
economic theory, and refers the reader to her empirical work on the
subject: *If You're So Smart: The Narrative of Economic Expertise* (1990).
She takes the opportunity to recognize an old guard of mathematical economist old enough to have known the Golden Age of pre-mechanistic or
pre-"scientistic" ([7][1]) economics. For example, Milton Friedman is quoted
saying, "the role of statistics is not to discover truth. The role of statistics is
to resolve disagreements among people" (4). This is then developed into
the observation that the actual *practice* of economics corresponds very
weakly with positivist declared methodology. She thus absolves all but the
relatively small community of economic methodologists of their rhetorical
sins.

We don't know what we're doing but – as supposedly remarked by Einstein – that's why what we do is called research. Since economists do not
actually follow any specific methodological strictures, our adhockery

allows us to side step the epistemological problems encountered by methodologists and philosophers of science. As an alternative to methodological criteria, McCloskey turns to what she calls the conversation of economics. The economic conversation as a new metaphor for economic science launches the study of rhetoric in economics as "a conversation about the conversation" (27). I will try to demonstrate with this text that this seemingly innocuous metaphor, when allowed to blossom, could have an immense potential to improve both our understanding and our practice of economics. At this point, it is not yet quite clear what level of inquiry McCloskey is referring to. Following Tarascio's (1975, 1997) approach it becomes evident that there are three levels to this metaphor: *economic activity itself* seen as a conversation between economic agents, *economic science* as conversation between practitioners of the dismal science, and what she later calls *economic criticism* as a conversation between a pluralistic group of polite and enlightened interdisciplinary scholars – the gymnasium of Athens. Each metaphoric level is determined by its degree of particularity: A conversation between economic agents can be about bond yields; a conversation between economists can be about the functioning of the bond market or about how to make predictions about bond yields; a conversation between economic critics can be about how appropriate are macro-models for policy proposals or about how and *why* such models have evolved. In this third level, the structural distinction would apply to the metonymical relation between theory and meta-theory.

The term *conversation* can, at first glance, seem deceptively simple: a multidirectional flow of ideas perhaps? The apparent simplicity dissolves once one examines the characteristics of the archetypal conversation of human inquiry and starts sliding along its more specific threads such as scientific conversation, and arriving eventually at the blossoming buds of specific debates. The conversational space is not a vacuum and the flow of ideas is superimposed on top of a complex socio-political topography where ideas are subject to many forms of manipulations both motivated and not. Sticking with my topographical metaphor, unmotivated manipulation would be much like a flow of water following a path of least resistance: for example, an economist that is entirely unaware of how limited his choices of testable hypotheses are within the context of his inquiry. Motivated manipulation would be the more obvious academic power-games in which ideas struggle to rise in the food chain of grants and publications.

The first step towards observing rhetorical activity in economics is recognizing the *dual of language and knowledge*: "facts are constructed by words" (41) and models are metaphors. Recognizing that language is endogenous to the scientific endeavor at all levels of inquiry allows McCloskey to discuss the modernist separation of science from art and to note that metaphor is common to both. Her discussion of mathematical metaphor in economics opens with a useful look at how metaphors are used, but stops short of going beyond very basic notions of motivational speech from John Austin (1962) and John Searle's (1970) *Speech Act Theory* from which she will draw later. McCloskey's reluctance to seriously accost the most treacherous issue of the *workings* – as opposed to prevalence – of metaphor in science carries both a cost and a benefit. The benefit is that in satisfying herself with just observing the abundance and power of metaphor in economics texts she leads a successful attack on the methodological foundations of economics while maintaining traditional analytic coherence (i.e. making sense), and thus not alienating her intended readers. The cost is more complicated: Conversing about conversation in economics is not like conversing about economics. The two conversations exist on different levels of inquiry in terms of their object of investigation and their context; this is the difference between science and the science-of-science. But it gets worse: There is a terrible analytical feedback created whenever one tries to analyze language because the object-language (under investigation) is necessarily contaminated with the subject-language underlying one's analysis and even one's thoughts. Language is inescapable and ideas cannot be non-rhetorical in the sense of being language-neutral.

Brave attempts at building fundamental models of language (Formalism and Semiotics) revealed only more complications as the language of investigation found it increasingly hard to catch-up with the language it was investigating. This same problem was encountered by participants in the Vienna Circle in the 1920s. The Logical Positivist attempt at the development of a philosophy that applies logical analysis to the study of positive (or empirical) sciences established what was valid scientific knowledge according to its *method* (logic) and *scope* (context). Interestingly enough, the circle's initial criteria were primarily *rhetoric*: the cognitive significance of statements. I will argue throughout this text that perhaps the most successful attempt to investigate the structure and function of language in a rigorous way is that of the notorious French philosopher Jacques Derrida.

I do not imply nor expect that many economists should take the time and effort to read Derrida's impenetrable prose any more than I would recommend reading the theoretical macroeconomist Thomas Sargent's equally impenetrable mathematical prose to philosophers; the investment required is prohibitive. Those of us who seek to dig deeper into the issues raised by McCloskey and other contemporary economic philosophers – whether favorably or not – can no longer avoid this investment. As McCloskey admonishes, it is indeed time to do our homework on literary criticism.

What is literary or critical theory?

Critical theory is a very heterogeneous group of works that probably have little more in common than having the power to make strange the familiar and to make readers conceive of their own thinking, behavior, and institutions in new ways ... [T]heir force comes – and this is what places them in the genre I am identifying – not from the accepted procedures of a particular discipline but from the persuasive novelty of their redescriptions.

(Culler, 1982: 9)

Why have these theories developed ostensibly in and around literature violating the deeply rooted modern dichotomy between the arts and the sciences? Perhaps over its long history, literature and the theory thereof have evolved to be inherently more adept at dealing with problems of reflexivity and meta-communication – the contemporary theoretical angst – than analytical philosophy. This stems more from literature's social role than from any specific ontological or epistemic characteristic. In addition, literature has produced and still is producing a significant body of work on the problems of infinite regression, which are a major problem for analytical philosophy.

Within the general field of literary criticism, there is a problematic distinction between structuralism and post-structuralism that has parallels in the modern/postmodern distinction in philosophy. Most of the current ideas loosely defined as "critical theory" are typically placed under the post-structuralist banner.

[S]tructuralists take linguistics as a model and attempt to develop "grammars" – systematic inventories of elements and their possibilities of combination – that would account for the form and meaning of literary works; post-structuralists investigate the way in which this project is subverted by the workings of the texts themselves.

(Culler, 1982: 22)

Culler uses two characteristics to define post-structuralism: It is *uncanny* in a Freudian sense, and it is *rhetoric* in a classical sense. The uncanny is a crucial concept for Sigmund Freud. He defines it as "that class of the frightening which leads back to what is known of old and long familiar ... [T]he frightening element can be shown to be something repressed which *recurs*" (Freud, 1953–74, vol. 17: 220, 241). Culler observes that "though the uncanny is a violation of order, the unsettling mystery of an uncanny moment in literature or in criticism is the manifestation of a hidden order" (Culler, 1982: 24).

Finally, let's dispose of the notion that *post hoc ergo ultra hoc* with regard to the issues surrounding the pesky suffix "post-," which seems to have been appearing everywhere like mushrooms after the rain. Post-structuralism or post-modernism do not replace or transcend structuralism or modernism in any logic of hierarchy much as the uncanny does not replace or transcend the canny. The logic needed to make sense of these differences is the *logic of supplementarity*, which is a key concept for Derrida and will be discussed in detail later.

Readings and interpretations – the focus shifts

The focus on reading and interpretation is a common thread among modern critics. In a famous passage, the literary critic Roland Barthes heralds the demise of authorial sovereignty when he announces in his *Image, Music, Text* that

> [T]here is one place where [a text's] multiplicity is focused and that place is the reader, not, as was hitherto said, the author. The reader is the space on which all quotations that make up a writing are inscribed ... A text's unity lies not in its origin but in its destination ... The birth of the reader must be at the cost of the *death of the author*.
>
> (Barthes, 1977: 146, 148, emphasis added)

This approach has a long history: In his *Poetics*, Aristotle classifies tragic plots with reference to the effects they have on the audience. This practice was prevalent in the Renaissance and the Enlightenment as well and only declined with nineteenth century essentialism and romanticism.

Feminist critique is perhaps the most influential application of this heightened attention to readers and their interpretations. It is, after all, the study of the operation of reading with a *specific hypothesis of a reader in mind*. In the case of feminism, this hypothesized reader corresponds to probably the broadest possible human category: sex. This is what puts it in an excellent location from which to examine reading in general. Feminist theory seen as a case study of the problematic aspects of reading as a woman sheds light on the functioning of the implied reader in a text. Reading is always done with an implied hypothesis of a reader and there is always a gap or division within reading. Recognizing this gap between the *actual* reader and the hypothetical reader through which he reads, Stanley Fish (1980: 15) employs the concept of "interpretive communities" as a structure for different readings underlying his *Reader-response theory*. In effect, he shifted the gap from within the act of reading itself to the contextual borders that lay between different interpretive communities. This fragments the hypothesized or implied reader but maintains local stability of interpretation within the communities. Fish's move is a familiar one to economists who routinely struggle with problems surrounding the aggregation of individual actions into broad social movements.

Having problematized authorial control, one finds that the reader's control over reading is anything but unambiguous and is, as I hope to show, a critical issue for rhetoricians of science. The philosopher of semiotics and novelist Umberto Eco looks at a text's structure for its degree of openness. A "closed work" has a tight structure that presents itself to the reader with little need for input while the "open work" with its seemingly loose structure is open to many interpretations and requires creative input from its reader. The catch is that while closed texts have a more constrained set of possible interpretations, they easily lend themselves to multiple uses and applications. Counter intuitively, open texts are excellent vehicles for authorial manipulation because the text resists certain interpretations while facilitating others as a component of its structural strategy. Eco writes:

> Those texts that obsessively aim at arousing a precise response on the part of more or less precise empirical readers
>
> …
>
> are in fact open to any possible "aberrant" decoding. A text so immoderately "open" to every possible interpretation will be called a *closed* one. You cannot use the [open] text as you want, but only as the text wants you to use it. An open text, however "open" it be, cannot afford whatever interpretation.
>
> (Eco, 1981: 8, 19)

Reading this paragraph with the hypothesis of an economics-instructed reader, one may consider the metaphors of a closed or open macroeconomic model as an illustration. Closed macro-models view the economy as a closed national system while open macro-models attempt to account for international interdependencies. A *closed* macro-model allows for the generation of more results while an *open* macro-model is less theoretically supple due to the particular relations it must specify.

Texts resist being pinned down by critics, and language resists theories that attempt to master it. Control is thus *fluctuating* between the reader and the text. These complications do not only inhibit the lofty realms of poetry and philosophy but are prevalent even with the simple joke. *Reader-response theory* would claim that it is the reader of the joke who determines the structure and meaning of the utterance. This is simply because a joke is not a joke unless it produces laughter in the listener/reader. Freud's theory of *Witz* (wit) complicates things:

> And yet this decisive action of the third person [laughing or not] lies beyond all volition – one cannot will to laugh – and outside of consciousness, insofar as one never knows, at the moment of laughter, what one is laughing at.
>
> (Weber, 1977: 25–6, in Culler, 1982: 72–3)

It would seem that no one controls the joke. The author certainly does not since his conscious joke may not be funny to the reader or, alternatively, an utterance he did not intend to be funny is found to be hilarious by the reader. Freud and Weber then show that even if it is the reader's reaction to the utterance that qualifies it as a joke or not, he too is not in control of the joke since its effect is often involuntary. The only remaining option is that the joke – the text – is the only potential controlling agent in this exchange.

Various theories of reading examine the impossibilities of establishing fundamental distinctions between a text and its reader, and between facts and interpretations. A theory of a single force, source, or system from which all particular instances devolve (*monism*) emerges because everything collapses into interpretation. Fish (1980: 165) finds himself obliged to admit that he cannot establish what it *is* (ontologically) that interpretation interprets. Stories of reading, on the other hand, are inherently *dualistic*, and are precisely concerned with the question Fish cannot answer. Stories are metonymical entities that have a structure of contingency: reader–text, interpreter–interpretee, and subject–object in the case of science. In order to escape the debilitating effects of the above monism, we will need to understand deconstruction.

What is deconstruction?

First, of course, one must note that deconstruction takes many guises, and that many of them seem almost contradictory to Derrida's work. The confusion arises because deconstruction is neither a theory of reading nor a story of reading; it is a *strategy* of reading. Furthermore, it is a philosophical strategy that operates with and on self-referenciality in reading philosophy itself. In an interview, Derrida defines a general strategy of deconstruction:

> In a traditional philosophical opposition we have not a peaceful coexistence of facing terms but a violent hierarchy. One of the terms dominates the other (axiologically, logically, etc.), occupies the commanding position. To deconstruct the opposition is above all, at a particular moment, to reverse the hierarchy.
>
> (Derrida, 1972/1981: 56–7/41)[2]

Elsewhere he elaborates on the strategic aspect of this reversal and explains that deconstruction should,

> through a double gesture, a double science, a double writing, put into practice a *reversal* of the classical opposition *and* a general *displacement* of the system. It is on that condition alone that deconstruction will provide the means of *intervening* in the field of oppositions it criticizes and which is also a field of non-discursive forces.
>
> (Derrida, 1977a: 195)

Derrida wants this strategy to intervene not only within philosophy's logical structure but also, and above all, within its strategic structure of power.

> To "deconstruct" philosophy is thus to work through the structured genealogy of its concepts in the most scrupulous and immanent fashion, but at the same time to determine, from a certain external perspective that it cannot name or describe, what this history may have concealed or excluded, constituting itself as history through this repression in which it has a stake.
>
> (Derrida, 1972/1981: 15/6)

Culler carefully reduces Derrida's fragmented definitions to the following simple proposition:

> [T]o deconstruct a discourse is to show how it undermines the philosophy it asserts, or the hierarchical oppositions on which it relies, by identifying in the text the rhetorical operations that produce the supposed ground of argument, the key concept or premise.
>
> (Culler, 1982: 86)

To illustrate this reversal procedure while taking note of the genealogy of Derrida's work itself, Culler uses Friedrich Nietzsche's deconstruction of causality in *The Will to Power* (1888):

> The fragment of the outside world of which we become conscious comes after the effect that has been produced on us and is projected a posteriori as its "cause". In the phenomenalism of the "inner world" we invent the chronology of cause and effect. The basic fact of "inner experience" is that the cause gets imagined after the effect has occurred.
>
> (Nietzsche, 1888, in Culler, 1982: 86)

In deconstructing causality, or anything else for that matter, one is *relying on the very principle one is deconstructing*. In this case, Nietzsche's argument against the logical and temporal priority of cause over effect is itself entirely founded on the concept of logical and temporal priority. He applies causality to causality itself in order to undermine the accepted hierarchy of cause and effect. Many critics of deconstruction have argued that it is nothing more than a modernized version of David Hume's skeptical argument in his *Treatise of Human Nature* (1739–40). Hume states that the only observable form of causality one can experience is "that like objects have always been placed in like relations of contiguity and succession." Deconstruction goes further than debunking the philosophical foundation of the concept of cause. Culler shows that it is in fact *fundamentally* different in the structure of its argument.

This double procedure of systematically employing the concepts or premises one is undermining puts the critic in a position not of skeptical detachment but of unwarrantable involvement, *asserting the indispensability of causation while denying it any rigorous justification.*

(Culler, 1982: 87–8, emphasis added)

By showing the possibility of reversing the logical and temporal hierarchy in which the effect is supplemental and subordinate to the cause, one is studying the rhetorical operation that established the hierarchy in the first place. This is the second gesture of deconstruction in which the reversed hierarchy is reinserted into the system it supports. This system is inevitably structurally displaced by the reversal – a vaccination of sorts against metaphysical beliefs. It is important to note that reversal and displacement are achieved *within* the logical context of the disrupted system. Deconstruction eschews the metaphysical need to replace one hierarchical opposition with another once the former shows signs of not being able to serve as an absolute foundation for thought. It is in this ability and willingness to engage its object within the context of its own metaphysical foundations that deconstruction is fundamentally an internal criticism compatible with any *form* of human thought.

Derrida has spent much time and effort looking at the relationship between writing and philosophy. He defines these very broadly to include any systematic field of study: a discipline and its discourse. Any discipline attempts to solve problems it encounters on its way towards explaining – at least part of – the world. At least potentially, issues can be put to rest once the practitioners of the discipline get it right. Writing is thus perceived as a byproduct of the activity of knowledge-production that – in the best of all possible worlds – should be as transparent and rare as possible. This view has been confronted with the fact that the more authoritative an interpretation, the more writing it generates. In economics, we are particularly aware of continuing debates over fundamental aspects of our theories that should have been resolved by now if ideas could indeed be separated from the texts in which they are embedded. The philosophy of economics is thus either non-progressive in the (Lakatosian) sense of moving in the general direction of the truth; or it cannot dominate its rhetoric dimension; or, as I suspect, both.

We have a hierarchical opposition: idea over text, which should be examined with reference to the long tradition of viewing writing as inferior to speech and philosophy. This tradition can be traced from Plato in the *Phaedrus* through Saussure's semiotics to Austin and Searle's speech-act theory.

What law governs this "contradiction," this opposition to itself of what is said against writing, of a dictum that pronounces itself against itself as soon as it finds its way into writing, as soon as it writes down its self-identity and carries away what is proper to it *against* this ground of

writing? This "contradiction," which is nothing other than the rela-
tion-to-self of dictum as it opposes itself to scription.

(Derrida, 1981: 158)

Allow me to translate the Derridian vernacular with the help of the indispensable Jonathan Culler:

> It is precisely because it is written that philosophy must condemn
> writing, must define itself against writing. To claim that its statements
> are structured by logic, reason, truth, and not by the rhetoric of the
> language in which they are "expressed," philosophical discourse
> defines itself against writing.
>
> (Culler, 1982: 91)

The problem lies in the mediation between thought and its forms of expression. Speech has the advantage of maintaining the link with the *origin*: the
thinker. In semiotics, the sign is composed of a *signifier*, which is an arbitrary
word, symbol, or sound that refers to a *signified* non-arbitrary meaning.
Though speech, like writing, also uses arbitrary signifiers, these are not
allowed to fester in the text and can be clarified by the speaker. Writing, on
the other hand, is physically detached from the origin of the ideas it is supposed to convey, thus empowering rhetoric manipulation. *Phonocentrism* –
the view that speech is privileged over writing due to its closeness to the original idea expressed – leads to *logocentrism*, which is philosophy's orienta-
tion toward an order of meaning conceived as a foundation existing in itself;
the traditional concept of reason (*logos*). For Derrida, the search for a foundation is the uniting characteristic of *all competing philosophies*.

Logocentric systems of hierarchical oppositions (e.g. content/form,
science/art, soul/body, literal/metaphorical, nature/culture, serious/non-
serious, etc.) are structured as a superior term whose high presence
belongs to the logos (reason), and an inferior term defined in relation to
the superior as a supplemental special case and seen as a fall (in the theological sense). Logocentric analysis is defined by Derrida as

> the enterprise of returning "strategically," in idealization, to an origin
> or to a "priority" seen as simple, intact, normal, pure, standard, self-
> identical, in order *then* to conceive of derivation, complication, deteri-
> oration, accident, etc. All metaphysics have proceeded thus, from
> Plato to Rousseau, from Descartes to Husserl: good before evil, the
> positive before the negative, the pure before the impure, the simple
> before the complicated, the essential before the accidental, the imi-
> tated before the imitation, etc. This is not just *one* metaphysical
> gesture among others; it is the metaphysical exigency, the most con-
> stant, profound, and potent procedure.
>
> (Derrida, 1977b: 236)

This metaphysical system gives structure to all rational thinking. Concepts such as clarifying, grasping, revealing, etc. all refer to a supposed literal or metaphorical presence. The Cartesian *cogito ergo sum* (I think therefore I am), for example, relies on the idea that the self can avoid doubting its existence because it is *present* to itself in the act of thought.

On the psychological level, Derrida finds evidence of the same inevitable presence. The privilege of the *phonè* (the sound of speech) does not depend upon a choice that might have been avoided had society followed a different evolutionary path. *S'entendre parler* (hearing oneself speak) is the experience of simultaneously hearing and understanding oneself as one speaks, which is different from the experience of hearing another voice, decoding the signifiers, and understanding the signified meaning. When we speak, signifiers seem to efface themselves before the signified concepts, which thus appear to emerge spontaneously from within the self as fully formed ideas. This experience of the effacement of the signifier in voice is not one illusion among others. Because it combines the possibility of objectivity through a constant meaning present in numerous appearances, with dominance of meaning over appearance, "it is the condition of the very idea of truth" (Culler, 1982: 108). The system of "hearing/understanding-oneself-speak" establishes consciousness as self-presence and presents itself as a non-exterior, non-worldly, and therefore non-empirical signifier. Arising from the difference between the outside and the inside, it has necessarily dominated the history of the world during an entire epoch, and has even produced the concept of the world. The idea of the world is the idea of the real: that which is *outside* consciousness.

My reading of Derrida places him apart from most others who espouse post-modernism. This is because he is arguing that the metaphysical system of hierarchical oppositions underlying the realist/relativist debate and human inquiry in general is in fact *necessary for rational thought*. It is necessary not as a crutch we can now finally discard in order to embrace a new epistemic paradigm that will lead us to some form of holistic knowledge. On the contrary, Derrida views reason and its metaphysical foundations as humanity's greatest edifice that should be studied *within* its context.

Division: the inconsistency of economic methodology

McCloskey presents Science with a capital S as an absolute and thus metaphysical version of actual science. The difference is that Science seeks the Truth (again capital letter means absolute) while science seeks truths – plural and relative. The enormous implication of the basic tenant of relativism is left to fester without explicit attention. McCloskey does however use an illuminating metaphor when she compares "Scientism" (from Friedrich Hayek's 1942–44 "Scientism and the Study of Society") to an orthodox religion (66). Scientism refers to methodological dogma – the politics of science – not science in use. Its adherents are obsessed with increased specificity and improved tools in an attempt to develop methods of inquiry in which objective-sterility is maintained despite external subjectivity. In the process they, as August Comte himself realized early on, are obliged to develop a scientific mystique to insulate their work from *themselves*. Readers of Comte would be correct to argue that his realization was actually only that the lay masses will require an alternative mystique to replace traditional metaphysical systems (such as religions) in order to serve the church of science. My interpretation of the strategic function of the cult of humanity within Comte's polity does not depend on any explicit recognition by the author. Comte may have intuitively sensed the need for a metaphysical foundation at the core of any analytical system but lacked the Derridian vocabulary to articulate it. Whatever the case may be, I hold that a metaphysical foundation is necessary for any system of knowledge from classical positivism to political correctness.

At this point McCloskey presents the linguistic distinction between *metaphor* and *metonym* with the basic economic concepts of *substitutability* and *complementarity* (between goods and services). She is of course explaining the concepts of metaphor and metonym to an intended reader who is an economist by way of an economic metaphor. This is a particularly elegant persuasion device: A concept from a foreign discipline is introduced via a highly familiar concept and thus acquires justification through it. The reader's delight with the deep understanding only possible with a familiar concept makes him more susceptible to persuasion – a point made by Adam Smith in the *Theory of Moral Sentiment*. This however does not violate her commitment to *sprachetik* since it facilitates understanding, and is not devious but illustrative of what speech-act theory designates as *motivated speech-acts* which are, as their name suggests, acts of speech which are uttered in order to perform a social action such as persuade. She continues by laying out what she calls the "rhetorical tetrad" (62) in a simple table (Table 2), representing the basic relationships between fact, logic, story, and metaphor. Here too we have the appeal to Greek authority in the context of an Anglo-Saxon academia.

Now that the schematics are laid out, the idea of reading economics to criticize itself – economic criticism – is established on an *ethical* basis. As with other dimensions of her text, McCloskey introduces an ethical dimension in its use and not at some fundamental level. This is an empirical rhetoric approach in that the readers are first invited to call on their own experiences as practicing economists and only later are confronted with some of the philosophical, methodological, or indeed political implications of economic criticism. The three *columns* of economic criticism – allow me to indulge in Greekism too – address the three inconsistencies in modernist methodology of economics:

Table 2 The rhetorical tetrad (adapted from McCloskey, 1994: 62)

Fact		Story (metonymy)	Particularity,	Empirical
From induction		From understanding	closeness	British
			↑	
			Axis of	
			particularity	
			↓	
Logic		Metaphor	Generality,	Logical
From deduction		From abduction	similarity	French
	Axis			
Impersonal	← of →	*Personal*		
	impersonality			
Scientific	← The →	Humanistic		
Male	Modernist	Female		
Numbers	Dichotomy	Words		
Precise		Intuitive		
Hard		Soft		
Truth		Opinion		
Objective		Subjective		
Cognition		Feeling		
Science		Arts		
Business		Pleasure		

Theorem of intellectual modesty – "if you're so smart" (71)

This is the primary focus of McCloskey's *If You're so Smart: The Narrative of Economic Expertise* (1990) and refers to economics' inability to meet its own criteria for success, illustrated by problems with prediction and forecasting. It raises the question of how economists cling to a methodology that has little practical reference or applicability to the daily business of economics. The immediate implication is, of course, methodological pluralism.

Maxim of intellectual exchange – "economist, perform thy trade" (74)

Modern economics can be seen as having gone through thirty years of *specialization without trade*. The drawbacks of such a practice come straight out of Adam Smith and certainly constitute a well-respected entry in the discipline's Canon. Using this economic metaphor establishes McCloskey's call for diverse and interdisciplinary work in economics – that's the trade – along with increased specialization.

Paradox of persuasion – "talk is not cheap" (76)

McCloskey's empiricism prompts her to observe the functions of talk in the economy itself. There is a need for an economics of talk because talk plays an important role in the economy. She presents empirical data that overall suggests that a full quarter of the labor force is primarily devoted to persuasion. It seems illogical and even foolhardy to disregard this in most economic models. Some work on this has been done in the transaction-costs tradition launched by Ronald Coats in the 1930s (see also various texts by Richard Nelson and Sidney Winter). McCloskey does not pursue this issue but it is an excellent example of the influence exerted by positive methodological constructs on the actual practice of economics. It is hardly surprising, after all, that a Scientist who believes that True Knowledge is arrived at by maximizing a specific type of content under a specific set of constraints, would attribute the same sort of rational behavior to economic agents. If persuasion has no role in True Science, why would it have a role in the market?

McCloskey distinguishes between "thin" (85) and "thick" (94) ways of reading economics. The thin is represented by the different variants of positivism and modernism, while the thick is comprised of ethics, economics, sociology, and rhetoric. Thickness as a philosophical term refers to the degree to which the domain of questions is restrained. McCloskey recognizes (again) the importance of thin readings in economics, but goes on to point out an inherent weakness in the Lakatosian (see above) view of progressive science progressing towards the Truth (with a capital T). She employs a classical rhetoric device called *petitio principii* (begging the question; literally: petition of the principals) in the following way: The principle of falsification *begs the question* falsification of what? In addition, a hypothesis of the form: "Is model X applicable in this case?" is irrelevant to economic questions. The logic of Lakatosian progressiveness is flawed if economics is to function as a *science* and not as *mathematics* since it involves an ontological (or existential) tautology: Science is *defined* as a system of models satisfying the ontological criteria of some renowned methodologists. Thick readings would allow themselves to follow their scientific curiosity wherever it may take them. "Good science is not good method; it is good conversation" (100). Whether these conversations are judged relevant and interesting to economics will depend on economists and their rhetoric. Furthermore, this is neither radical nor unique, and has been the underlying process by which mathematical economics itself has reached the level of prestige it now enjoys.

McCloskey then fires the first round in a battle she picks up later with epistemology. She quotes the philosopher Rom Harré:

Neither falsehood nor truth is an attainable epistemic ideal. [Epistemic ideals] are proper only for the moral exhortation and castigation of a community of seekers after trustworthy knowledge.

(Harré, 1986: 95)

Proof: the style of mathematical formalism

"The rise of a scientistic style" (111) is the name of the chapter opening McCloskey's *proof*. She presents a statistical-historical study (as a prominent economic historian her credentials are obvious) of articles in economics journals from the early twentieth century and up to the present. She then conducts a rhetorical critique based on her "rhetorical tetrad" (see Table 2 above). She finds that papers have essentially maintained a similar ratio of theoretical to empirical, but that the quantity of mathematical expressions has increased tremendously over the years. At this point, it would be useful to introduce a literary definition for a term McCloskey uses: *implied author*. It refers to the literary persona of the author that is implied by the text and the reader's interpretation of it, the point being that the difference between journal articles *before* this Great Mathematization and *after* it is a difference between implied authors. I have arranged her distinctions in table form (Table 3).

McCloskey proceeds to uncover some of the rhetorical devices found in modern economic jargon. When macroeconomists use words like "perfect foresight" or "time-inconsistency problem" there is a whole layer of connotations in the mind of the reader (*hypotext* is the literary term) consisting of what these words signify for people who understand them – perhaps in different ways. McCloskey introduces another literary term: *implied reader*. In this case, he would be the persona of the economist reading these papers as implied by the text. This is not necessarily the same as the *intended reader*, who would be the reader *consciously intended* by the author. For successful persuasion, modern economic papers make sure that the *implied* reader corresponds to actual *intended* readers' aspirations: these days usually a math-whiz. The implied author should not however be intolerable so the use of language such as "may lead to ..." "tends to ..." and "suggests ..." has risen accordingly. The removal of the first person "I" from most academic narratives is of course a crude stylistic device used to give the implied author an objective aura. There is an entire set of academic *styles* because style is interrelated with context, and academic discourse is conducted according to different stylistic codes for different hierarchical levels of texts: personal distribution, working papers, journal articles, speeches, conferences, rewritten doctoral dissertations, or interdisciplinary manuscripts. The fact of the adaptability of style to its *perfor-*

Table 3 Different implied authors in economic literature

	Theoretical – logic/metaphor	*Empirical – fact/metonym*
Then	Philosopher – scholar	Historian – scholar
Now	Mathematician – theorem and proof virtuoso	"Bench-scientist" – technician

mative role and context can be used to demonstrate the falsity of the style–content opposition.

McCloskey then turns specifically to the rhetoric of mathematical formalism and particularly its obsession with existence theorems. She makes the distinction between science and mathematics, the latter characterized by the predominance of axiomatic existence theorems based on stylized facts where data is relatively ignored. In this light, she claims that "physics is less mathematical than modern economics" (129). This is where the increased mathematization of economics bothers McCloskey. Affirmations of existence theorems of the form: "there exists a solution such that assumption A holds" are irrelevant if the question has to do with finite cases under assumptions A' or A" close to A but not actually A. "For that question you need approximations and simulations and empirically relevant parameters, not existence theorems" (134).

McCloskey also notes that the entire *rigor* in these papers is only applied to the math – the text's deductive process – while the opening and conclusions are left arbitrary and vague. Examples include choice of assumptions based on aesthetics: "more realistic" without empirical justification, "less restrictive" to manipulations not applications. Formalist economists should be surprised to be accused of applying their entire disciplinary rigor to the *style* of their work (mathematical) instead of its *substance* (economics). The consequence of this practice is that exact results with restricted applications are produced over approximate results with wide applications; or, in the jargon of the philosophy of science: low empirical content. "[T]he procedure of modern economics is too much a search through the hyperspace of conceivable assumptions" (137). McCloskey illustrates this flaw with a *metatheorem* (a theorem about theorems; see Figure 1).

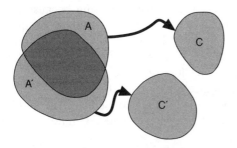

Figure 1 Metatheorem on Hyperspaces of Assumptions for each and every set of assumptions A implying a conclusion C and for each alternative conclusion C' arbitrarily far from C (for example, disjoint with C), there exists an alternative set of assumptions A' arbitrarily close to the original assumption A, such that A' implies C'. (Source: McCloskey, 1994: 138.)

Investigating mathematical economic models within the rhetorical value system of mathematics is *not* falsification. There is a need for a quantitative rhetoric of approximation with which scientists can address the questions of "how large is large?" and "how close is close enough?" if science is to refer to something else but itself. The problem is not the *use* of logic and math but *formalism*, which depends on the rhetoric of existence theorems. Therefore, it is actually mathematical economics and not rhetorical analysis that adheres to the "anything goes!" anti methodological credo.

McCloskey views formalists as poets and politicians. Mathematical economists are thus formalist poets, while modernist methodologists are formalist politicians. The formers are in an aesthetic pursuit of consistency that is not particularly relevant to science, and the latter are "scholastic not scholarly" (171). She concludes her proof with the observation that "the usual graduate program takes intelligent young people and makes them into idiot savants" (173). Ouch.

Refutation: the problems of epistemology and truth

Even if the evil Methodologist (with a capital M) and Co. may recognize that social dynamics – conversation in the broad sense – are more relevant than Positivist dogma in the evolution of the science, they remain uncomfortable without an *epistemological foundation*. This is a very ancient angst that can be traced back to Plato: The Socratic *elenchus* was a *rhetoric* technique by which True Knowledge is justified with *elenctic* argument which, it should be noted, is not a refutation on logical grounds but a critical *cross-examination* (the literal meaning is in fact *shaming*). McCloskey (1994: 188–9) follows Gregory Vlastos (1991) in pointing out that Socrates (via Plato) implicitly assumes that Truth (absolute, with a capital T) resides somewhere in his interlocutors' own belief system. This critique seems deceptively straightforward and is part of McCloskey's attack on epistemology. "The very idea of epistemology" (title of the first chapter of the refutation) is repugnant to her. This is not surprising because this is where she gingerly avoids directly addressing the problem of theory-choice. One need not even apply radical French criticism to see this. In 1866, J. S. Mill observed that "The dogmatic Plato seems a different person from the elenctic Plato." McCloskey could have noted this and used it to examine the epistemologically complex relation between logic (the dogmatic Plato) and conversation/persuasion (the elenctic Plato) which underlies and undermines *both* what August Comte and later Jacques Derrida called metaphysics.

McCloskey feels obliged to respond to the typical *tu quoque* (you also) circular argument that permeates much of the discussion in the trenches of the realist–relativist debate, and has been circulating for several millennia. In this instance, the debate takes the form: "in asserting the truth of relativism you acknowledge a standard of truth – gotcha!" (The use of "gotcha" is McCloskey's.) She paraphrases Uskali Mäki's (1988a and b) definition of realism as meaning that a world exists independent of our perceptions of it. She remarks that,

> if "our perceptions" are taken to mean "the perceptions about which we speak to each other, testing by conversation their mutual reasonableness and freedom from illusion," then I am a realist, and so is every working scientist.
>
> (McCloskey, 1994: 203)

She argues that since science is based on previous science, realism is a rhetorical necessity for accumulation of knowledge – a "performative of trust" in the parlance of speech-act theory (Harré, 1986: 90). It is not Truth but "the truth made rather than found" (211) that is the goal of science. This would make theory choice based on truth not a problem: "it is a matter of the practical rhetoric of experiments, for example, to decide whether gravity waves are true or not" (211).

She quotes the linguist and logician James McCawley (1990): "Reason does not establish that a conclusion is true, but at most that it involves no errors beyond those that one is already committed to" (207). Derrida looks at those commitments as a structure holding a web of meaning together. This meaning is co-relative to all participants' views (multi-subjective) yet approximately stable in a specific context. This stability can accommodate the elusive concept of scientific objectivity. The problem of reality independent of perception can be traced back to the Greeks whose arguments have been refined over the past 2500 years but have essentially remained unresolved. McCloskey views epistemology as human inquiry's most prolonged failure. She adopts a pragmatic position and argues that the problem of reality is a non-issue, which is not only a waste of time but detrimental to scientific practice. The pragmatic solution is to discard the basic definition of truth as some sort of correspondence with what *is*, in favor of viewing truth as dependent on a system of justification – what John Dewey called "warrantable assertion" (Rorty, 1980: 176).

The rich multidisciplinary discourse between realists subscribing to the correspondence theory of truth and pragmatists with their relative and institutional definition of truth exhibits an intriguing paradox. Realists defend their view on pragmatic grounds: The existence of a real albeit unattainable truth is necessary if inquiry is to have a point; while pragmatists claim that the truth *is* a social construct and *is not* absolute. Each side defends a view with arguments whose logic contradicts the view they are defending: pragmatic realism/absolutism versus absolutist relativism/pragmatism. This paradox may have arrested the functioning of the epistemological conversation in economics.

Paradoxes are vintage locations from which to look at the systems they violate because they are true yet contradictory or inconsistent. They bring the structure of reason to the surface because they violate the system's logical structure using the very logic they violate. The paradox can thus be seen as a naturally occurring deconstruction, which displaces the difference *between* realism and relativism *into* realism and relativism via their discourse. This should become clearer after looking at several paradoxes and inconsistencies arising in various theoretical contexts including semiotics and speech act theory, that are relevant for my discussion. Once again, let's start with the Greeks who – at least symbolically – represent the dawn of western rationality which is perhaps as broad a context as even Derrida would venture to examine.

Zeno was an early deconstructor in his study of paradoxes. The familiar paradox of the impossibility of motion is demonstrated by the flight of an arrow. Culler shows that this paradox is only paradoxical *because* it is presented within a metaphysical system of *presence* which views reality as what is present at any given instant. He proceeds by deconstructing the paradox using its own presence/absence opposition to displace its system of reality. At any given moment, the arrow is in a particular point and never in motion. Nevertheless, we all know that the arrow *is* in motion! In Nobel laureate economist Robert Solow's words: "It is a pity to have to make this commonplace point. But how else can one deal with this sort of foolishness?" (Solow, 1988: 32). Yet the arrow's motion is never *present* at any moment; hence the paradox. The paradox is not the arrow's; it is cheerfully moving, ready to penetrate the heart of any skeptic that stands in its way. The paradox is in our conception of the real as what is present at any given instant as a simple, indecomposable absolute. The past is a former present, the future an anticipated present, but the present instant simply is: an autonomous given. The presence of motion is conceivable only insofar as every instant is already marked with traces of the past and the future. Motion can be realistically conceived only if the present instant is not something given but a product of relations between past and future. Something can be happening at a given instant only if the instant is already divided *within itself*, inhabited by the non-present. This structural paradox can now be used to explain my claim that the difference *between* realism and relativism has been displaced and disseminated *into* realism and relativism via their discourse. The paradoxical justifications they offer expose truth's persistent self-reflexive duplicity which is marked by traces of the outside (reality) and the inside (interpretation). The traces relate to each other via mutual presupposition, not social consensus as the relativists hold, nor correspondence as the realists would have it.

McCloskey accuses the Methodologists of imposing the goal of Truth seeking on a speech community of working scientists who engage in truth seeking: "a rhetorical conversation, socially constructed and factually constrained" (216). Lower case-t truth seeking requires training because of the need to join in the conversation of the economics speech community. I mentioned before that such communities are based on a shared *hypotext*, or the web of shared connotations that are the foundation of meaning. The word foundation here is used *very* loosely since it is obvious such shared connotations are very fluid. Philosophers are thus not qualified to pre-scribe to working economists because they do not understand the conver-sation and thus disregard the *practical* importance of truths. Methodologists fail in the philosophy of their science if they fail to recog-nize that

> every set of metaphysical or regulative principles that have been sug-gested as necessary for science in the past has either been violated by subsequent acceptable science, or the principles concerned are such that we can see how plausible developments in our science would in fact violate them in the future.
>
> (Mary Hesse, 1980: x, in McCloskey, 1994: 217)

McCloskey uses the orthodox distinction between science and art to argue that the metatheorem A=>C and A'=>C' (see above) is not science but mathematics. It seems she is implying that mathematics is an art with scientific applications. Such a view could apply in different degrees to other disciplines including economics. Once again, she is accepting the importance of artistic devices such as general equilibrium theory in so far as they enrich the conversation conceptually. The degree of *applicability* – though not mentioned directly – is emerging as the McCloskian criteria along with the Habermasian *sprachethik* that she adopts. Precisely *not* anything goes: "I'm a conformist" (272) conforming to rhetorically expressed criteria.

There are thus two heuristics maintaining the essential balance between continuity and progress – a balance that is central to Kuhn and Lakatos. Social construction assures a degree of continuity because academic insti-tutions adjudicate on theory and meta-theory based on rhetoric conven-tions that, in turn, rely on coherence with the commonly held views of the intellectual elite. Factual constraints can foster progress through the intro-duction of anomalies that shift paradigms, and by constraining certain dis-course (redundant or counterfactual) from being added to the archive of knowledge. The question of how factual constraints are imposed socially within a rhetorical conversation is not addressed by McCloskey in this sur-prisingly conservative "growth of knowledge" model. The same logic however, reapplied to this inductive heuristic of progress, would show that factual constraints themselves are used for the socially constructed rhe-torical adjudication process within the institutions that make up the archive.

With regard to the question of the goal and domain of rhetoric-analysis, McCloskey prescribes empirical investigations of *what* persuaded econo-mists over time, theoretical models of *how* economists are persuaded, as well as evaluating the theories themselves. She draws a parallel with literary criticism addressing both style and structure of a text and *assessing* it as well. Rhetoric analysis can help in "erecting standards of assessment" (197). Following McCloskey's line of reasoning, these standards will have to be contextualized within specific speech communities.

She observes that rhetorical certitude in social science is particularly dangerous since "planners and politicians, believing themselves in sight of utopia, are encouraged to ordain. It is not an encouragement they need" (296). As usual, McCloskey finishes a chapter with a well-glossed paragraph most of the intended audience would find hard to disagree with: "oh well, if the consequence of these philosophical ramblings on rhetoric is an affirmation of good-old libertarianism, then all the best to them!" This is quite familiar really and is an appeal to A=>C and A'=>C' in that the intended reader finds that this bewilderingly new A' implies C after all – how comforting not to have to deal with an alternative outcome C'.

A. W. Coats (1987: 305–7) writes that crude modernist methodology should now be viewed as a dead horse and thus no further flogging is necessary. McCloskey however justifies continuing the flogging by pointing out that the horse is in fact *un-dead* and roaming the halls of economics departments. She then uses Platonic dialogues to engage her major critics in an effective campaign of zombie horse flogging. This image links beautifully to one of my favorite McCloskey metaphors:

> The "discipline" [of modernism] doesn't bite in practice. Modernists talk a lot about "discipline" and "rigor" and "compelling proof," in a vocabulary approaching the sadomasochistic, but when it gets down to the whips and chains they don't carry through.
>
> (McCloskey, 1994: 310)

"Shamefully, I have not read more than a page or two of Gadamer or Derrida" (315, emphasis added). With this apology, McCloskey launches a polite attack on deconstruction with its main thrust being that it is no more than Greek rhetoric with French flare and exuberance. McCloskey's reading of deconstruction is primarily based on a single (albeit interesting, innovative, and even brave) paper dealing with deconstruction and economics: Jane Rossetti's "Deconstructing Robert Lucas" (1990, 1992). I shall therefore take McCloskey *seriously* when she writes that she has "tentative objections to deconstruction, which can only be taken seriously when I get down to work and *do the homework I have not yet done*" (McCloskey 1994: 329, emphasis added). I'm happy to report that since writing *Knowledge and Persuasion* she has done her homework and is now unapologetically postmodern while maintaining an appreciation of the long cyclical history of relativism and deconstructive practices in the history of ideas. She has however left the explicit homework assignment for her readers and I'm delighted to submit them with this text.

Hermeneutics are however "just what I would recommend" and she quotes fragments from the historian of economics Philip Mirowski's characterization of the pragmatic tradition in the philosophy of science that I reproduce here:

1   Science is primarily a process of inquiry by a self-identified community, and not a mechanical legitimation procedure of some pre-existent goal or end-state. Science has conformed to no set of ahistorical decision rules, and for this reason history and science are inseparable. Most of this would come under the rubric of Dewey's "instrumentalism."

2   Possible methods of inquiry consist of deduction, induction, and abduction [metaphor]. No one method is self-sufficient without the other two as complements. Abduction is the explicit source of novelty, whereas induction and deduction provide checks and balances.

3   There is no single logic, but rather a logic of abduction, a logic of deduction, and a logic of induction.

4   Because there are no foolproof impersonal rules of scientific method, decisions concerning the validity of scientific statements reside within the community of inquiry. The community of inquiry is the basic epistemological unit.

5   Without a strict mind–body duality, science has an irreducible anthropomorphic character. This is not inherently a dangerous phenomenon. Natural laws themselves evolved, as do the members of the community of inquiry. Social and natural concepts interpenetrate; therefore hermeneutic techniques are a necessary component of scientific inquiry, on the same epistemic level as mathematical techniques.

6   The study of semiotics and interrelation of signs constitutes an integral part of the philosophy of science.

7   Because pragmatism must ultimately depend upon the community of inquiry, the Scylla and Charybdis it most frequently must negotiate between are a defense of the *status quo* and an advocacy of technocratic utopia.

(Mirowski, 1990: 94)[3]

McCloskey continues to illustrate these versions of Marx's theory of ideology with a barrage of examples from different sources both empirical and theoretical, such as the following quote from Nietzsche:

[Formalism depends on] a movable host of metaphors, metonymies, and anthropomorphisms: in short, a sum of human relations which have been poetically and rhetorically intensified, transferred, and embellished, and which, after long usage, seem to a people to be fixed, canonical, and binding.

(Nietzsche, 1870, in McCloskey, 1994: 337)

She concludes with a chapter reiterating the moral dimension of the rhetoric of economics defined with reference to personal rhetorical consistency. So economics lacks integrity and is immoral because the declared method does not cohere with the practice. This, I venture to suggest, resembles bourgeois virtue less than it does Talmudic morality.

Peroration

The metaphor of the economy *itself* as a conversation is finally addressed. McCloskey starts by drawing attention to the parallel linguistics of "relative value" (368) in the works of Léon Walras at Lausanne and Ferdinand de Saussure in Geneva, founders of general equilibrium theories in economics and Semiotics in linguistics respectively. McCloskey is referring to the analogy between language and prices in their information-carrying capacity. Semiotics' basic model of meaning is comprised of an arbitrary *signifier* such as the word "sky" that refers to a *signified* concept such as the atmosphere viewed from Earth's surface. The theory also recognizes that the value of words and expressions does not stem entirely from the ideas and concepts they signify but also from the *relative values* of different signifiers within the text. One has only to consider what the actual English signifier "sky" can signify in different contexts to appreciate this problem.

She then introduces speech-act theory more explicitly, stressing the economically appealing view of language as motivated by its power to *produce* actions. This is not unlike game theory's moves. Speech-act theorists (especially John Searle) have focused on reducing the complexities of language, motivation, and meaning to a series, albeit exhaustive, of categories of speech-acts. An example of the potential use of a speech-act framework could be looking at the division of labor as "limited by the extent of the talk" (372) because increased levels of specialization require increased levels of talk between specialities.

What Noam Chomsky called language communities are commonly seen as based on social convention. An example used by McCloskey is Wayne Booth's concept of a stable irony, which refers to the context in which a specific irony is perceived as such. A language community can thus be defined according to which utterance (a suitably broad term) is perceived as ironic or not. I am delighted that McCloskey has neglected to use the following: Milton Friedman's proposed "3 percent rule" for monetary growth. This rule is ironic to a language community of economists who are versed in the *hypotext* (recall: underlying contextual connotations) of the problem of moral hazard and expectations in macroeconomic policy which could be called the "discretion versus rules literature." Simply put, the argument for rules is that if you want monetary stability you need to bind yourself by a strict rule or else you will be tempted to intervene, and people will expect you to do so. Only in this context would being *per-*

suaded by Friedman's utterance make any *economic* sense as an acceptance of the structural superiority of rule-based monetary policy. It makes *political* sense however on metaphysical – dare I say voodoo – grounds. Irony however rarely survives the mangle of politics.

McCloskey calls on us to examine communication explicitly as an economic phenomenon and presents empirical evidence (surveys[4]) that talk is important in explaining fluctuations in the stock market. It turns out that most decisions are based on re-processed information in the form of advice. Her critique of economics as focusing almost entirely on the individual subject with almost complete disregard to social interaction and relationships is evocative of the great economist Vilfredo Pareto's critique of economics in his rarely read *Trattato di sociologia generale* (1916).

Finally, one arrives at the last chapter, "The consequences of rhetoric." Economic criticism is at a very early stage and is a work-in-progress by definition. She answers the impending *So what?* with which economist-philosophers are often confronted by reminding the economic mathematicians of the days when they faced similar questions. "The question of what matters in scholarship can be answered only by attending to the conversation of the scholars who decide" (380). She then re-appeals to empirically overwhelming rhetorical elements in economic science. Economic criticism will facilitate communication with other language communities: both academic and lay. This could mitigate the evolutionarily counterproductive incestuous effect of ever more restricted language communities.

Rhetorical devices have been and are used implicitly in economics and could be exposed with McCloskian inverse hermeneutics. By inverse hermeneutics, I mean that while hermeneutics peels off layers of context to expose and study the truth at the core, reverse hermeneutics does the same in order to study the layers of context. Rhetorical analysis could eventually introduce argumentative standards that could help settle arguments in economics. After all, if falsification was such a decisive methodological tool why are there so many old and unsettled disagreements about fundamental economic phenomena?

McCloskey then explains how the empirical models based on macro-economic models are *wrong* due to variables specified incorrectly as endogenous yielding biased and inconsistent fitted coefficients; she is comfortable in her econometric authority here. She seems to reproduce textually the familiar pedagogical movement in which the professor leans back in her chair with a calm paternal smile on her lips, ready to embark on an office-hour lecture to a beloved student. She concludes the paragraph with the following statement: "Modern macroeconomics is erroneous. (Don't get mad: think about it.) The theorizing is misinformed and therefore irrelevant to an economy in a world. The empiricism is wrong" (388).

Politicians and the media – and hence public opinion – are influenced by economists and their rhetoric. McCloskey ventures that "The costs in policies unrealistically imposed has probably amounted to tens if not hundreds of billions of dollars, all from a merely rhetorical mistake" (390). She then gets angry:

> the standards of "consistent theory" or "good prediction" presently in use are low to the point of scientific fraud (again Blaug said it well in 1980). They are six-inch hurdles over which the economist leaps with a show of athletic effort. A non-rhetorical economics has low argumentative standards.
>
> (McCloskey, 1994: 392)

This concludes my rhetorically self-conscious reading of Deirdre McCloskey's *Knowledge and Persuasion in Economics* (1994). It attempted to present her argument in a concise way that is reflective of the original in style and structure. After discussing Uskali Mäki's analytical reconstruction of McCloskey's underlying philosophy in the *Division* below, I will discuss some of the contemporaneous debates surrounding the literary and critical theory from which McCloskey has drawn. These interdisciplinary newcomers to economics are obviously relevant to a serious understanding of the rhetorical issues she has introduced into our field. This however is complicated by the fact that McCloskey spends very little time explicitly presenting the literary, linguistic, and philosophical underpinning of her work. This is not necessarily a bad thing since it allows her to steer a steady and relentless course to the heart of the issues at hand without a lengthy and potentially distracting excursion into the more technical aspects of critical theory.

3 Division

The Mäki diagnosis

Context

Probably the most interesting and fruitful response to McCloskey's rhetoric was the economic philosopher Uskali Mäki's series of critiques focusing primarily on his specialty: realism. These include "How to Combine Rhetoric and Realism in the Methodology of Economics" (1988a), "Realism, Economics and Rhetoric: A Rejoinder to McCloskey" (1988b), "Two Philosophies of the Rhetoric of Economics" (1993), and finally "Diagnosing McCloskey" (1995), which came right after McCloskey's *Knowledge and Persuasion* (1994). The diagnosis includes and refines Mäki's major arguments, and has the advantage of having a direct response by McCloskey in the same issue of the *Journal of Economic Literature*: "Modern Epistemology Against Analytical Philosophy: A Reply to Mäki" (1995a). Since I intend to proceed with a close reading of one representative text, the diagnosis seems ideal.

Mäki opens with a very friendly tone, thanking McCloskey for her discussion and draft comments on what was to become his "Two Philosophies of the Rhetoric of Economics" (1993). He notes the confusion with which McCloskey's work has been received, and proposes to *rationally reconstruct* – an interpretative endeavor – her underlying philosophical ideas. Mäki briefly mentions the study of the rhetoric of science and the "new" rhetoric to point out that "McCloskey's version can be understood only in the context of the specific conundrums of its subject, economics, and the background of general intellectual currents" (Mäki, 1995: 1301). Unless stated otherwise, all page references in this section are from Mäki's "Diagnosing McCloskey" (1995).

As an illustration, Mäki argues that "McCloskey's views offer themselves as a successor to Friedman's famous methodological strictures in the 1950's" (1301). This is an interesting *rhetorical* argument that performs its stated pedagogical aims admirably. Understanding the relationship between McCloskey's and Friedman's respective philosophies – as well as the specific genealogy implied by the concept "successor" – requires a multifaceted approach. Mäki leaves the details to the reader but I would briefly mention some of the common threads that must have entered into his consideration: The most obvious is that McCloskey and Friedman share a *political* affiliation as (old-school) Chicago, laissez faire economists. The example then takes an implicit rhetorical turn when it functions as a hypotext (subtext) to Mäki's eventual evaluation of McCloskey's work. Unlike his economics, Friedman's methodological instrumentalism (the view that predictive ability supercedes realism of assumptions as a criterion for theoretical validity) is widely regarded as wanting philosophically, methodologically, and empirically (since economists are awful predictors). His 1953 paper has however enjoyed a level of attention that is disproportional to its contribution and is in fact the single most quoted methodological/philosophical paper in economics. With his little illustration of the importance of placing his subject in the "context of the specific conundrums of its subject, economics, and the background of general intellectual currents" (1301), Mäki fires the first volley in his exchange with McCloskey before the actual hostilities even begin. I suspect that it is the brunt of this *rhetorical* critique, and not the diagnosis itself, that irked McCloskey into her relatively abrasive response (see below).

Mäki states that his goals in this essay are to "dispel some of the prevailing misunderstanding" with a

> clarification and partial reconstruction of McCloskey's views so as to make their presuppositions and implications clearer than they have been in his and his commentators' writings ... On the other hand, the clarification unavoidably turns into a critical diagnosis. It appears that there is something in need of a diagnosis, something that is not quite all right; the clarification reveals that McCloskey does not have an entirely unambiguous and coherent view of economics as rhetoric. This clarification and critique should make it easier for economists to reassess the attempted revolution, the project of viewing economics as rhetoric.
>
> (Mäki, 1995: 1301)

Mäki organizes his clarifying reconstruction along three axes: a concept of rhetoric, a theory of truth, and a "theory of the social organization of economics (presumed to be a market order)" (1301).

Concept of rhetoric

Mäki points out that this is a concept with a long and torturous history and that its interpretations can range from "eloquence of speech" to "the study of the use of symbols in general" (1302). McCloskey's reconstructed characterization of the concept of rhetoric first recognizes the "obvious distinction between rhetoric as linguistic practice and rhetoric as the systematic study of that practice" (1302). However when setting out to do the latter, McCloskey provides

> various fragmented and scattered characterizations which isolate a number of its possible aspects in terms of different primitive concepts; this may give the impression of an unorganized collection of partial characterizations ... To make sense of [her] position, we must gather these threads together.
>
> (Mäki, 1995: 1302)

The primitive concepts McCloskey uses to characterize rhetoric are conversation [R1], argument [R2], and persuasion [R3]. I am using Mäki's notations [Rx] in order to facilitate references to the original text and maintain the flavor of his analytics. Combining these three primitives yields [R4] to which he adds a "moral component ... often expressed in terms of *honesty* ... [arriving at] ... a rough definition of rhetoric in terms of persuasion, audience, argument, and conversation with a moral tone" (1303).

[R5] Rhetoric is the use of arguments to persuade one's audience in an honest conversation (and the study thereof).

From this perspective, rhetoric is a social process that involves
- [i] A persuader (speaker, writer);
- [ii] A persuadee or an audience (listener, reader);
- [iii] The aim of the persuader to persuade the persuadee;
- [iv] Argument as the means to attain the aim;
- [v] Honest conversation as the social channel of persuasion.

(Mäki, 1995: 1303)

This is then suggested as coming "very close to what McCloskey has tried to pursue.[4]" (1303, footnote in the original). Footnote 4 adds an implicit [R6] which Mäki chooses to *exclude* because it is "devoid of any specifications of the goals of language use ... it is not clear how it fits with the other characterizations" (1303, note 4). This is the first exclusion Mäki makes in order to support the concept of rhetoric; there are others that I will duly note and eventually explain below. He quotes McCloskey on this characterization: "Rhetoric is an economics of language, the study of how scarce means are allocated to the insatiable desires of people to be heard" (McCloskey in Mäki 1995: 1303, n4). [R6] could have been – in accordance with the reconstructive structure suggested by Mäki – specified as follows:

[R6] Rhetoric is the use of arguments to persuade one's audience in an honest conversation, which is *governed by conflict of interests and scarcity* (and the study thereof).

How to define an economics of anything in a single sub-phrase is a challenging reductive exercise that I shall leave to others. The list [i] to [v] (see [R5] above) could now include a new item:

> [vi]   Socio-political system of knowledge-production (an archive).

But Mäki is satisfied with [R5], and proposes to trim it down further with the following words:

> This notion of rhetoric is coherent. It is also very thick as it combines a number of different components. We next consider the concept of rhetoric formulated more thinly in terms of only [i]–[iv], that is, rhetoric in the sense of [R4].
>
> (Mäki, 1995: 1303)

Recall: "[R4] Rhetoric is the use of arguments to persuade one's audience (and the study thereof)" (1303). This (second) exclusion ends the section titled "McCloskey's Multiple Rhetorics" (1301) with the *elimination of the moral component* in the reconstruction of McCloskey's definition of rhetoric. It is thus surprising to find that it immediately precedes section 3: "Rhetorical Justification of Beliefs" (1303) which starts with the following paragraph:

> One is attracted by a rhetorical notion of the justification of economic theories and models if one accepts the following statements. Economic theories and models do not speak for themselves and against their rivals. Data do not speak for or against theories. Logic does not speak for or against theories. Economists speak for or against theories by appealing to data, logic, and a number of other things. Economists attempt to justify theories by trying to persuade their audiences.
>
> (Mäki, 1995: 1303)

He then directly proceeds to "clarify the implications for the idea of justification of the concept of rhetoric in the sense of [R4]" (1303). The reader will recall that [R4] involves persuasion [iii] and argument [iv].

Mäki's *persuasion* explicitly subsumes authorial intent: "More precisely, the aim of the persuader is to increase the intensity of the persuadee's belief in a statement" (1304). Mäki's *arguments* are reminiscent of semiotics and consist of two parts and a relationship between them: *premises* – that the persuader assumes are shared by the persuadee – *conclusions* – in which the persuader wants to intensify the persuadee's belief – and their *relationship*. The latter is left very broad and defined as a "connection" (rhetorical by definition, I would argue) between the premises and the conclusions "which the persuader assumes that the persuadee accepts or finds appealing. Typically, many elements of such an argument remain implicit" (1304). The path taken, or not, from premises to conclusions is not a simple one and could involve a multitude of very thick series such as logic (defined in various ways), empathy, pride, manipulation, fear, experience, pathos, etc. Mäki recognizes this as McCloskey's appeal for argumentative pluralism.

Mäki recognizes that persuasion is based on belief and manipulations thereof. "A belief is a property predicable of human beings in their relation to statements: people believe in statements" (1304). The relationship between statements and human beings is a relation of *plausibility*. He then specifically defines *rhetorical* persuasion as *"the transference of plausibility by means of arguments"* (1304). I am unsure as to what *non*-rhetorical persuasion may be, and why Mäki makes a point of excluding it. What is transferred is the plausibility (vis-à-vis the persuadee) of the premises to the plausibility (and thus enhancement of belief) of the conclusions.

Mäki defines coherence as characterizing the relationship between premises and conclusions. Like persuasion, argument too undergoes a specification, and the discussion addresses *rhetorical* argument (again, what is *non*-rhetorical argument? why the exclusion?). Coherence and plausibility relate as follows: "the increase in the plausibility of the conclusion is brought about by the coherence between the conclusion and the premises" (1304).

Before continuing, I would like to tentatively answer the "rhetorical" questions I posed above, concerning why Mäki defines persuasion and argument as specifically rhetoric. Is he implicitly excluding non-rhetorical persuasion and argument or is the adjective redundant? Since redundancy is generally all but nonexistent in Mäki's prose, it is possible that he uses the qualifying term "rhetorical" for emphasis. A more illuminating interpretation can be derived from the work of the philosopher Michel Foucault. He made a distinction between discursive and non-discursive structures that can shed light on the question of whether there are such things as non-rhetorical persuasion and argument. Following Foucault, non-rhetorical persuasion and argument are the *institutions* of persuasion and argument. Examples of non-discursive persuasion and argument could be the institutions of conferences, journals, tenure-tracks, email correspondence, or even the fish market. They are of course fundamentally tied to their discursive counterparts which are the actual texts that the institutions produce, debate, exclude, and edit as part of the processes of persuasion and argument. I will return to Foucault in *The Production of Knowledge* in the *Proof* below.

The groundwork is now in place for Mäki's diagnosis of McCloskey's concept of rhetoric:

> We are now ready to suggest that the acknowledgement of rhetoric in the sense of [R4] as rational amounts to accepting a *coherence theory of justification* (but not vice versa). By implication, this applies also to [R5], McCloskey's thickest version ... [She] is not only making a

descriptive point about how economists in fact adopt beliefs, but also that in so doing economists behave in a scientifically rational way.

(Mäki, 1995: 1305)

The implication is that *"all beliefs are justified by their relations to other beliefs with which they cohere ...* Coherence theory is thus in conflict with forms of what is customarily called foundationalism" (1305). Here of course is where analytical philosophy – necessarily foundationalist – is forced to reject the alien relativity of coherence theory. But Mäki is much too elegant and persuasive to resort to a vulgar *tu quoque* (or *gotcha* argument as McCloskey calls it) with regard to the problem of standards of justification or, closer to the disciplinary home of economist-philosophers, theory choice. The "solution" is then to add "specific constraints on the set of relevant beliefs," forming *"theories of the nature of plausibility.* All of these theories suggest that it is coherence constrained in a certain way that constitutes plausibility" (1305). This is the crux of Mäki's reconstruction of what McCloskey does with her definition of rhetoric. Specifically "It turns out that although [she] is extremely ambiguous about this notion, specifications can be suggested which are consistent with [her] notion of rhetoric formulated in [R5] [recall: rhetoric plus ethics but minus economics]." The trouble is that it "turns out that with these specifications, truth amounts to the same thing as plausibility" (1305).

Theory of truth

McCloskey's theory of truth is the source of the trouble but it is even harder to pin down than her concept of rhetoric:

> The problem ... is that we do not know what McCloskey means by "true" and by related expressions such as capital-T "True", "correct," and "right." [She] uses these expressions for making [her] case as if they delivered intuitively clear ideas. But they do not. *Unfortunately, they appear to have worked as persuasive tools*; many commentators have adopted the expressions without further question. While I was able to identify a coherent notion of rhetoric in [her] writing, I did not have similar success with [her] vocabulary of veracity.
>
> (Mäki, 1995: 1305, emphasis added)

There may be a revealing slip in the emphasized sentence in this passage. Why is McCloskey's persuasiveness unfortunate? Is it because it does not depend on a purely analytical conceptual structure of truth? Is this actually what Mäki meant when he made the implicit distinction between rhetoric and non-rhetoric persuasion and argument? If so, he is following in the steps of Plato in defining "real" philosophy in opposition to rhetoric (logo-centrism, see *Narration* above).

Mäki nevertheless proceeds by establishing an initial reference point: a *correspondence* theory of truth that he has suggested in his "How to Combine Rhetoric and Realism in the Methodology of Economics" (Mäki, 1988a: 97), and one to which McCloskey has explicitly consented in her "Two Replies and a Dialogue on the Rhetoric of Economics: Mäki, Rappaport, and Rosenberg" (McCloskey, 1988b: 150–66). Here are his analytical reconstructions:

[t1]   The truth (with small t) of a statement S consists in its correspondence with objective (i.e., S-independent) reality.

[T2]   The Truth (with capital T) of a statement consists in justified certainty about its truth in the sense of [t1].

(Mäki, 1995: 1306)

Mäki realizes that "contrary to [McCloskey's] admission regarding the notion of capital-T Truth, McCloskey has several other characterizations of it" (1306). Worse yet, McCloskey's most ubiquitous definition for capital-T Truth, was reformulated by Mäki in [T3] as follows:

[T3]   The Truth (with capital T) of a statement S consists in its correspondence with objective (i.e., S-independent) reality.

(Mäki, 1995: 1306)

According to Mäki, this reconstruction [T3] has the advantage that "No idea of certainty is implied" (1306). It is however the same as [t1] above. This radically undermines the differentiation between [t1] and [T2] and thus renders the distinction between the two concepts of truth based on the possibility of justified certainty useless for Mäki.

Mining McCloskey's rhetoric for other prose from which to suggest other "interpretive reformulations" (1306), Mäki quotes the following from McCloskey which, since it is crucial for his reconstruction, I reproduce in its entirety:

[T]here is a problem with Truth. The problem is not with lowercase truth, which gives answers to questions arising now in human conversations, requiring no access to the mind of God: On a Fahrenheit scale, what is the temperature in Iowa City this afternoon? ... You and I can answer such questions, improving our answers in shared discourse. The problem comes when trying to vault into a higher realm, asking whether such and such a methodology will lead ultimately to the end of the conversation, to the final Truth ... Questions such as "What will economics look like once it is finished?" are not answerable on this side of the Last Judgment.

(McCloskey, 1988c: 245–57, in Mäki, 1995: 1306)

Mäki notes that a correspondence theory of truth is no longer behind neither formulations of truth nor Truth. He proposes a new reformulation of small-t truth:

[t4]   The truth (with small t) of a statement consists in its coherence with a certain set of beliefs, that humans end up with in an ongoing conversation before the ideal limit of all conversation.

(Mäki, 1995: 1306)

There are two major characteristics differentiating [t4] from the initial [t1]: First, reformulated truth [t4] is based on a coherence theory of truth "because it makes truth dependent on beliefs and argument in a conversation rather than on the relationship between a statement and reality" (1307). Second, "truth [is] something that is *essentially attainable*" (1307). The problem, as McCloskey asserts in the passage quoted above, is with capital-T Truth. Mäki starts with [T5], which reads: "The Truth (with capital T) of a statement consists in its coherence with God's beliefs," but then gives it a "more profane face" (1307) as follows:

[T6]   The Truth (with capital T) of a statement consists in its coherence with a set of human beliefs reached as a result of human conversation taken to its ideal limit.

(Mäki, 1995: 1307)

Mäki thus arrives at two definitions of (lowercase-t) truth: coherent and correspondent, and two coherent *and* two correspondent definitions of (Capital-T) Truth. Furthermore, he points out that unlike the case of rhetoric ([R1]–[R5]) the definitions are not all mutually consistent and that they do not complement each other. Noting (in a footnote) that even this is not satisfactorily exhaustive, he proposes

to continue the clarification and reconstruction of McCloskey's views by adopting [t4] *as the most plausible specification of the concept of small-t truth* and [T6] *as the most plausible specification of the concept of capital-T Truth.* These two seem also to provide the best fit with the way that McCloskey characterizes the notion of rhetoric, as given by [R5].

(Mäki, 1995: 1308)

For the reader's convenience, I reproduce the definitions of [t4] and [T6] here:

[t4]   The truth (with small t) of a statement consists in its coherence with a certain set of beliefs, that humans end up with in an ongoing conversation before the ideal limit of all conversation.

...

[T6] The Truth (with capital T) of a statement consists in its coherence with a set of human beliefs reached as a result of human
conversation taken to its ideal limit.

(Mäki, 1995: 1306–7)

We now have a reconstructed McCloskey subscribing to both a coherent
theory of justification (rhetoric) and a coherent theory of truth (pragmatic). The implications are indeed radical:

> there is *no difference between the general character of plausibility and
> truth, or between that of justification and truth*. The question of the cri-
> teria of truth (the proper purview of a theory of justification) and the
> question of the concept of truth (the proper purview of a theory of
> truth) are conflated. Coherence constitutes both the criterion and the
> essence of truth.
>
> (Mäki, 1995: 1308)

Much like the move from [R4] to [R5], coherent theories of truth must
also impose constraints on permissible sets of beliefs; otherwise, any
theory constructed as a coherent system would be true. [R5] added an
ethical constraint: "honest conversation" for that purpose. At this point
Mäki ascribes no special significance to the fact that even in his own reconstruction, truth is *irreducibly* multiple and exclusions are the only way out
of this bind: The criteria he finds with regard to truth (defined by the pair
[t4], [T6]) is that of *attainability* which is a property of [t4] and *not* of [T6].
The relationship of attainability here can be readily deconstructed in a
way I hope would intrigue Mäki: We have a *differential* hierarchical
opposition based on human attainability. The direction of the hierarchy
would be [t4] before [T6] for McCloskey who privileges the former. But
also, occupying the same space, a *deferential* relationship or even criteria
emerges. This is because the notion of attainability is constructed as
depending on the *deferral* of human conversation to its final, ideal limit.
What just happened to Mäki's text is an auto-deconstruction in which the
conceptual structure emerges as that of difference and deferral – *différance* is Derrida's term.

Différance is probably the most well known Derridian term. He starts
with a term: difference (*différence* in French) that is well established in
modern philosophy and linguistics (a system of difference is central to the
works of Nietzsche, Saussure, Freud, Husserl, Heidegger, and many
others). He then silently deforms it into *différance*, which sounds the same
but is a verbal noun of the verb *différer*, which means to differ and/or
defer. *Différance* thus captures both the passive preexisting structures as
well as the active event of differing that produces them – a simultaneous
"toggling" (to use Richard Lanham's term) between event and structure.
Ferdinand de Saussure's semiotics laid out in his *Cours de linguistique*

génerale (1907) sees language as a system of signs whose function is to signify meaning. A speech-event is a signifier and the meaning it conveys by arbitrary convention is the signified. What defines a signifier is its difference from other signifiers, not its relation to its signified – onomatopoeia (e.g. buzzing) is perhaps the exception.

Saussure's semiotics harbor a paradox: that of *parole* (word: an event) and *langue* (language: a structure). The meaning of a word is given by the meaning assigned to them in prior speech. In fact, the same logic would lead to the conclusion that the whole structure of a language is produced by speech-act events. The "original" events that determine structures, are themselves determined by pre-existing structures that, in turn, are derived from prior speech-acts – a system of *infinite regression*. Even if we trace the grunt that conveyed to our primate ancestors the idea of "it feels good to eat!" to the very first time it was grunted, we would have to assume a prior structure that must at the very least establish that sounds emitted – the grunt – are linked to events experienced – fresh kill. Furthermore, this structure is a structure of differences. In this example, there are at least a few oppositions that could be mentioned: this specific grunt/other grunts, feeling good/feeling bad, eating/not eating, etc. Derrida writes:

> There is a circle here, for if one distinguishes rigorously *langue* and *parole*, code and message, schema and usage, etc. ... one does not know where to begin and how something can in general begin, be it *langue* or *parole*. One must therefore recognize, prior to any dissociation of *langue* and *parole*, code and message, and what goes with it, a systematic production of differences, the *production* of a system of differences – a *différance* among whose effects one might later, by abstraction and for specific reasons, distinguish a linguistics of *langue* from a linguistics of *parole*.
>
> (Derrida, 1972/1981: 40/28)

Social organization of economics

Now that the ground is prepared, we come to the principle thrust of the diagnosis when Mäki reconstructs McCloskey's scientific criteria. First there is the social constraint he calls an *"elite theory of truth"* which is formulated as follows:

> [t4^s]   The truth (with small t) of a statement consists in its coherence with a certain set of beliefs that a privileged set of humans end up with in an ongoing conversation before the ideal limit of all conversation.
>
> (Mäki, 1995: 1309)

Mäki disapproves of this approach not on humanist egalitarian grounds, but because there is an internal contradiction in McCloskey's thesis when she writes:

> We believe and act on what persuades us – not what persuades a majority of a *badly chosen* jury, but what persuades *well-educated* participants in the conversations of our civilization and of our field. To attempt to go beyond persuasive reasoning is to let epistemology limit reasonable persuasion.
>
> (McCloskey, 1985: 46, in Mäki, 1995: 1310)

Mäki suggests that McCloskey herself "goes beyond persuasive reasoning" in imposing social constraints that exclude the *badly chosen* and *badly educated* from the conversation. How can we be sure that the elite know any better than the rest of us? After all, nothing is said about how exactly this elite is constituted as such. I agree and so would McCloskey. But what would be the alternative? What constitutes a contradiction in the context of Mäki's analytics is actually the multiplicity typical of postmodern thought. The processes of academe are far from perfect but there is no philosopher's stone to determine the truth so we are stuck in the political world of dissertation committees and peer reviewers.

With this notion of what I would call *realpolitik* truth [t4^s] we are just a step away from a full-blown bourgeois virtue based on *sprachethik*; what Mäki calls an "*angel theory of truth*" reformulated below:

> [t4^m]   The truth (with small t) of a statement consists in its coherence with a certain set of beliefs that a privileged set of humans, obeying the canons of *Sprachethik*, end up with in an ongoing conversation before *the ideal limit of all conversation*.
>
> (Mäki, 1995: 1309)

Now all that is to be done to complete the reconstruction is to plug [R5] into [t4^m] as a characterization of a conversation obeying the canons of *sprachethik*, and *voilà*:

> *The conjunction of* [R5] *and* [t4^m] *gives a concise summary of my reconstructive interpretation of McCloskey's conception of rhetoric as persuasion aiming at morally and socially constrained plausibility.*
>
> (Mäki, 1995: 1310)

Mäki constructs the [t4^m] notion of truth as *herrschaftsfrei* coherence: "truth as dominance-free plausibility" (1311). To diagnose the concept of *sprachethik* Mäki introduces another Habermasian idiom as a plausible interpretation. Mäki reintroduces the supplementary (relegated to footnote 4) version of rhetoric to which I decided to award a full [R6] designation (see above) to reconstruct McCloskey's *herrschaftsfrei* social order. In Mäki's words – interlaced and echoing quotes that he *sprach*-ethically selects from McCloskey:

> the liberal market order ... Laissez fair is the right policy regarding this market, not methodological control ... Instead of methodological regulation from outside, economics can rely on the self-government by individual scholars obeying the dicta of *Sprachethik* ... Methodology and Epistemology spoil conversations; let's get rid of them.
>
> (McCloskey, 1988b, 1988c, and 1989a, in Mäki, 1995: 1311)

Whether consciously or not, Mäki performs a deconstructive move in the following paragraph:

> We have earlier cited Solow, whose concern was that McCloskey's metaphor of economics as an ongoing conversation (rhetoric in the sense of [R1]) is "too permissive." We have now seen that it is permissive in the sense that it suggests liberating economists from external methodological regulation. At the same time, developed fully in terms of rhetoric in the sense of [R5], McCloskey's metatheory is extremely impermissive in that it imposes severe moral and social constraints on conversation.
>
> (Mäki, 1995: 1311)

Here Mäki makes what I consider his most fruitful criticism: McCloskey *must* resort to constraining the rhetoric of small-t truth. This is in order to support the reversal of the hierarchical opposition underlying the debate on the problem of the real – in this case, coherent truth over correspondent Truth. I used the term *realpolitik* truth to describe Mäki's *elite theory of truth* [t4^s] together with the *angel theory of truth* [t4^m] and its insistence on a liberal market order. When coming in contact with politics (from the faculty lounge to public policy), *realpolitik* truth would readily turn into a moralistic *real-ethic* with all the dark connotations such a term brings to a humanist such as McCloskey – surely not what she had intended. Here is where Mäki's diagnosis operates in the realm of what McCloskey in her reply calls "modern epistemology" (see below). This is neither a "gotcha" argument nor analytical pointing-out-of-contradictions (though it may have started that way). This however is not developed by Mäki or other McCloskey commentators. Mäki's own deconstruction illustrates an important point: Deconstruction is a strategic rhetorical procedure that is an integral part of rational thought and its associated phenomena such as argument, persuasion, analysis, reconstruction, and diagnosis. Failing to fully appreciate this leaves the bone of contention which divides Mäki and McCloskey buried. At this point, it would suffice to uncover the postmodern reply to Mäki's diagnosis: There is no such thing as an emancipating *theory*, only emancipating *practices*. I will return to this in the *Peroration* at the very end.

In the next section, Mäki lists what he claims McCloskey is not. She is not an intellectual anarchist, nor a postmodernist, nor is she a realist defined as one who subscribes to a correspondence theory of truth. The first negation should no longer be problematic; the last is seen as McCloskey's problem and is the basis of the proposed amendments Mäki suggests in the following sections, and the middle one is misleading. Declaring McCloskey as not a postmodern (an error) may be good politics especially if defined as political correctness – she certainly does not subscribe to *that* offshoot of postmodernism.

McCloskey's early evaluations of mainstream economics were rather favorable, "implying that the major ingredients of the substance of mainstream economics are true in the sense of [t4^m], i.e., true or plausible or rhetorically justified in the sense of morally constrained coherence" (1313). McCloskey has since adjusted her early tactical evaluation unfavorably but Mäki is justified in calling the attention to her apologetic rhetoric when he observes that "If the moral constraint does not hold, as was to be expected, what purpose does McCloskey's angel theory of truth – i.e., [t4^m] – serve?" (1313). Since McCloskey admits and in fact stresses how abominable economics' record on *sprachethik* is,

> in what sense is it possible to state that economics is well off, given that strict morality was built into the notion of truth? If economists are not going to behave like angels ... does this turn McCloskey's small-t truth into yet another capital-T Truth, an unattainable utopia?
>
> (Mäki, 1995: 1313)

Mäki is describing here the auto-deconstructive structure in McCloskey's reasoning or, more precisely, reconstruction thereof. McCloskey criticized economic formalism for lacking a *quantitative rhetoric of approximation* (see McCloskey, 1994: 141–2) and thus unable to be operational in the real world. Here the tables are turned:

> McCloskey would like truth to be operational. But how would [she] operationalize it? How would [she] measure the degree to which the *Sprachethik* is observed? The only consistent method would be by checking whether meta-level statements about the degree to which the *Sprachethik* is observed are plausible in a morally constrained way. How should [she] measure the plausibility of these latter statements? Only by appealing to a morally constrained plausibility of an even higher degree. And so on, ad infinitum. An infinite regress becomes unavoidable, and truth is no longer operational.
>
> (Mäki, 1995: 1313)

Opting to reconstruct McCloskey based on the *elite theory of truth* [t4ˢ] instead of the *angel theory of truth* [t4ᵐ] is open to the same criticism because of the problem of *selecting* the elite. I would suggest that using the supplementary characterization of rhetoric as an economics of ideas [R6] could help explain the rise and decline of elites. Having articulated the most influential and contested policy criteria in economics, Vilfredo Pareto set his talent to work elsewhere. He effectively argued that a formal economics, which cannot accommodate a more relevant criterion than "if somebody wins and nobody loses, go for it!" needs to develop a sociological foundation if theory is to become relevant to policy. Pareto developed a theory of an "elite-cycle" in a section of his voluminous *Tratato di Sociologia Generale* (1916). Much as I did not do justice to "Pareto optimality" earlier in this paragraph, I will be brutally brief here and direct the reader to the work of my teacher Vincent Tarascio on Pareto[1]. Pareto's theory of elites starts with the historical observation that strong "combinatory" tendencies in a social group lead to their ascendance through social, economic, and political innovations. Their success however leads to the strengthening of their conservative tendencies as they try to maintain their position as an elite. This inherent reduction in adaptability leads to their inevitable decline and the rise of another social group that is more adaptable. This is essentially an argument based on social evolution, an example of which would be the decline of the aristocracy and rise of the bourgeoisie. This extension could enhance what Mäki calls McCloskey's *elite theory of truth* [t4ˢ] but a reconstruction based on such an augmented [R6] and [t4ˢ] could not escape auto-deconstruction either – *no rational idea can.*

The final diagnosis and prescription follow:

> [Her] *own normative assessments of the ways of economics fail to be supported by* [her] *metatheory of economics.* [Her] *assessments must have some other metatheoretical basis which* [her] *rhetorical meta-theory fails to explicate* … In order to help McCloskey avoid at least some of the above problems, I suggest a simple remedy: *drop both elites and angels from your theory of truth as well as from your concept of rhetoric; give them a role at most in your theory of justification.*
>
> (Mäki, 1995: 1315)

Mäki's suggestions are indeed simple and come as something of an anticlimax in the narrative. Removing ethics (angels) and politics (elites) from both the concepts of truth and rhetoric – working with [t1] and [R4] for those who are still keeping track – in order to reduce thick readings to make them more consistent and operational is somewhat of a philosophical "cop-out" and is surprising in such a carefully crafted text. Keeping the concepts of truth separate from the concept of plausibility solves all of the technical problems raised by Mäki *but at the cost of reducing*

McCloskey's work to triviality. In the name of being operational – implicitly defined as non-contradictory – Mäki reduces the meta-conversation about the conversation about economics to the level of a weak defense:

> Thus, the *Sprachethik* may be a useful means for attaining truths and for measuring the degree to which truths have been attained, even if it leads into problems if incorporated into our definition of truth.
>
> (Mäki, 1995: 1316)

McCloskey's reply to Mäki

McCloskey's reply appeared immediately following Mäki's diagnosis and was titled: "Modern Epistemology Against Analytical Philosophy: A Reply to Mäki" (McCloskey, 1995a). It takes the form of a Socratic *elenchus* but, as always, with a touch of *sprachethik* to temper the inherent aggressive and condescending tones of such a cross-examination. McCloskey appreciates "the care and sympathy with which Uskali Mäki has read my books" and observes that overall "his reading is notably accurate. I've had worse readers. Much ... I agree therefore with most of what Mäki says" (McCloskey, 1995a: 1319). She agrees, for example, that her definitions of rhetoric are "fragmented and scattered" (Mäki, 1995, quoted in McCloskey, 1995a: 1319) but argues that they are "justifiably fragmented and scattered, as Mäki agrees" (McCloskey, 1995a: 1319). Whether Mäki *explicitly* agrees with this justification is not specified but the paragraph that follows sheds some light on the supposed – and perhaps only – agreement:

> "Rhetoric" is a word like democracy or freedom or capitalism, a complicated matter not easily fitted onto a 3 × 5 card. It is an essentially contested concept, which concerns half of our intellectual culture since the Greeks. Unlike some readers, Mäki has troubled to become acquainted with the other half.
>
> (McCloskey, 1995a: 1319)

Therefore, there is agreement that the subject matter at hand is complicated, old, and difficult; a traditional *Sprach*-ethical back-slapping that usually degenerates quickly into slapping *tout-court*.

The metaphor of fitting complex ideas onto a 3″ × 5″ card undoubtedly refers to Mäki's [R1]–[R5] and [t1]–[T6] reconstructive series and thus implicitly accuses Mäki of over-reduction. The rest of the quoted text is a little more confusing with its reference to *half* of our intellectual culture. Which half of whose intellectual culture is concerned with rhetoric, and what other half has Mäki acquainted himself with? The simple story could be that we are discussing Western intellectual culture, and that rhetoric is a concern of the latter half of hierarchically opposed concepts such as science/art, fact/fiction, substance/form, etc. Mäki thus is admirable as a scholar operating in the former half (analytical philosophy's domain) who is willing to go slumming with the "other half" (i.e. modern epistemology that operates in the latter or rather in both halves). McCloskey's disagreement with Mäki is on the latter's project of *assimilating* the uncanny modern epistemology into analytical philosophy:

> Where we disagree is on analytical philosophy. In a nutshell, Mäki wants to go on with a project of analytical philosophy *c.*1955 that most professionals now think is dead. I by contrast would like to move beyond it, as would many recent philosophers, worldly and otherwise.
>
> (McCloskey, 1995a: 1319)

McCloskey repeatedly dates Mäki with her reference to the year 1955 (no less than six times in this brief text). She appeals to authority in declaring at least Mäki's version of analytical philosophy dead. As often is the case, McCloskey is launching a double-pronged attack here. First, Mäki's diagnosis itself suffers from an epistemological contradiction because it uses inappropriate tools such as reconstructing primitives and locating contradictions for a meta-theoretical discussion of a complex and essentially contested concept such as rhetoric. At the political level – in the broadest sense of a strategic agenda – he is *aggressively helping* McCloskey's own agenda by offering her what can be seen as a *gift*[2] of a "consistent and operational reconstruction" along the lines of "analytical philosophy *c.*1955."

McCloskey specifically takes issue with the principal hierarchical opposition underlying Mäki's critique: correspondence *over* coherence theories of truth. She describes the opposition's deployment as follows:

> Having analyzed the definitions of truth into two sorts, the philosophers of 1955 and now Mäki make a strange rhetorical move: "O.K.: choose between them. Go ahead. You must."
>
> (McCloskey, 1995a: 1319)

She then argues that correspondence and coherence do not have to be "mutually consistent" (McCloskey 1995a: 1319, "mutually consistent" is the term used by Mäki) and that, in fact, they are used simultaneously in scientific argument. McCloskey demonstrates this in Mäki's diagnosis:

> Mäki uses correspondence to extract true statements about my writings; and the notions he is able to extract will depend on coherence with what he already believes – for example, about epistemology.
>
> (McCloskey, 1995a: 1319)

Mäki's definition of a *realist* as someone who believes only in a correspondence theory of truth is the foundational center of the argument according to which McCloskey is not a realist. McCloskey retorts that like many other people who call themselves realists, she does not hold *only* a coherence theory of truth.

> I hold both coherence and correspondence theories (and while we're at it, 20 other theories: the vocabulary of persuasion is richer than one plus one). I don't see why scientists can't hold both, or 22, and yet remain free from hassling by old-fashioned analytic philosophers for being "inconsistent."
>
> (McCloskey, 1995a: 1320)

McCloskey's puzzlement over Mäki's "strange rhetorical move" (McCloskey, 1995a: 1319, quoted above), in which he insists that correspondence and coherent theories of truth are mutually exclusive, has now taken a more aggressive tone. She points out that the imposed choice is between two versions of small-t truth: [t1] based on correspondence or [t4] based on coherence in Mäki's reconstruction, and that her God-metaphor for the transcendental Big-T Truth is misunderstood by Mäki. Unfortunately, McCloskey does not offer further information concerning this misunderstanding and concludes the part of the reply that addresses the reconstructive elements in Mäki as follows:

> It is therefore not surprising to conclude, as Mäki does after some analytical heavy lifting, that Big-T Truth is not the same thing as small-t and that I don't think much of Big-T. (The reason I don't think much of it, incidentally, is its use for aggression.)
>
> (McCloskey, 1995a: 1320)

The incidental remark in brackets alludes to Mäki's diagnosis of McCloskey's preference for small-t truth as due to its "essential attainability" (Mäki, 1995: 1307), and is perhaps a clue for understanding Mäki's misunderstanding. The point – as I deconstruct it – is that a relationship of *deferment* (in time) underwrites the concept of attainability, which is built into his reconstruction of McCloskey's concept of small-t truth and Big-T Truth. That, in turn, is what leads him to found his argument on the *differential* relationship between correspondence and coherence. Though no deconstructionist, Mäki does employ an implicit deconstructive move of his own when he shows how McCloskey is forced to erect *social* foundations for her concepts of truth in the absence of strict epistemological foundations. The apparent incommensurability and thus futility of Mäki and McCloskey's Wittgensteinian language-game makes way for interesting insights into alternative modes of rhetoric once a self-reflexive deconstructive reading is applied.

"After these philosophical preliminaries, Mäki turns to my sociology of knowledge. He tries to convict me of an anti-democratic delight in an 'elite'" (McCloskey, 1995a: 1320). McCloskey underplays the *realpolitik* of her concept of the socially constrained economics conversation but does not answer questions concerning the emergence and social dynamics of the inevitable elite.

> All I have in mind is that the people speaking in a conversation of science are often worth listening to when a scientific assertion is at issue. I don't see how else we can decide whether a scientific assertion is true ... Mäki quite properly emphasizes that my sociology becomes ethics when it turns to normative issues, such as what standard of persuasiveness an economic scientist should use. Again, I don't see how else we can talk about normative issues except by introducing norms ... Mäki sneers at the introduction of ethics – an "angel theory of truth," says he. He calls it "optimistic" and "utopian." ... That's what ethical talk is, and ethical talk permeates the scientific world. If you don't think so have a look at the latest controversy over cold fusion or over the elasticity of demand for health care ... Correspondence and coherence are too simple a vocabulary to describe scientific persuasion.
>
> (McCloskey, 1995a: 1320–1)

Evaluating scientific standards on shaky moral practices that are evidently utopian is problematic for Mäki, and for myself I must add. Mäki's concerns take the form: "Your theory is begging the question: How can we have ethical standards in an unethical world?" As she did with the problem of the elite, here too McCloskey disregards the specific – albeit multiple and complex – roles of ethical standards in her sociology of knowledge. She replies that

> the *petitio* is on the other *principium*. Mäki says that for the truth of my argument the economists must be observed acting ethically – "strictly." ... If it were not for the word "strictly" his charge of inconsistency would not work ... In other words, it is Mäki, not McCloskey, who builds his conclusion into his premise, by inserting that word "strictly." His claim that I have indulged in a *petitio principii* is erroneous. He himself has indulged in it. Philosopher analyze thyself.
>
> (McCloskey, 1995a: 1321–2)

Has the discussion finally deteriorated to a series of *tu quoque* arguments or even an exchange of what McCloskey calls "gotcha" arguments? She cannot perhaps be accused of violating the strictures of *sprachethik* as such, but her prose usually adheres to higher standards of discourse-*esthetics*. My reading of McCloskey however, suggests that once again she is employing a high degree of rhetorical sophistication even here. The tirade of analytical nit-picking she directs at Mäki is a caricature of his *Diagnosis* itself. Her message being that such exchanges are philosophical and scientifically sterile.

"A rhetorical theory of truth is a theory of small-t not Big-T truth; only in a Big-T world is it inconsistent to claim *Truth* for the absence of Truth" (McCloskey, 1995a: 1322, emphasis added). McCloskey is addressing the standard philosophical argument that relativists believe in a universal Truth which holds that there is no universal Truth – gotcha! The fault in this argument is that it only holds in a "Big-T world" which I would interpret as Mäki's philosophical position. Resorting to exclusions however does not serve McCloskey's argument well. It suggests that their philosophical positions are incommensurable. One could dispose of the exclusion by simply replacing the emphasized word "*Truth*" (in the quote above), with "truth." With this correction (t instead of T), her argument is a crucial one on which the entire postmodern edifice depends: The concepts of inconsistency and paradox are *contextual* like any concept and should be studied as such. In this case, Mäki would be correct in refuting the validity of a claim for universal non-Truth ("*Truth* for the absence of Truth") but that is *not* McCloskey's claim! Truth can be claimed consistently within a specific context, which can be very broad, and universal Truth is no more than a specific contextual truth with *metaphysical* delusions of grandeur. In this case, McCloskey's epistemological claim is that Truths are inevitably socially constructed from truths, and thus it is quite consistent to claim *truth* (not Truth) for the absence of Truth. Analytically this is because Truth-claims are always reducible to only a subset of an infinite set of truths. Science goes about its daily business of producing truths-in-context, while *exclusively* analytical philosophers defend a useless ideal. I would take the logic of the argument further: This ideal (Truth) is significantly more worrisome than McCloskey's angelic elites who preside over the conversation of science. This is because universal Truth must master its *entire* domain of truths in order to establish its Truthfulness. It is fundamentally at odds with *sprachethik* in that it is *by definition* territorial and imperialistic.

The last disagreement is with the contradiction Mäki finds in claiming both that *sprachethik* is not observed, and that economics is "in a pretty good shape."

> He [Mäki] wants me to offer philosophically acceptable reasons for saying it is [in pretty good shape.] But I am a simple economic historian and cannot offer philosophy to prove such a thing. I offer merely the evidence of my writing and reading on economic history and the teaching of price theory. I think that's where you judge whether economics is in good shape, out in the labs and libraries, not in the philosopher's study.
>
> (McCloskey, 1995a: 1322)

Again, McCloskey is resorting to exclusions that do her a disservice. There is good reason to criticize analytical philosophy for its will to dominate the entire contextual domain (see above) but that is no justification for assaulting it with a similarly territorial claim. Much can be learned about the functioning of economics in "the philosopher's study."

In conclusion, McCloskey reiterates that "Mäki wants to go on with the old program of epistemology before 1955, the program of finding Big-T Truth independent of history or society or ethics." Incidentally, this would be the *fifth* time 1955 is mentioned. She appeals to several philosophical authorities – Bruno Latour (1984) and Hilary Putnam (1990) – including a strong paragraph from William Rozeboom's "Why I Know So Much More Than You Do."

> No harm will be done, I suppose, by retaining a special name for true beliefs at the theoretical limit of absolute conviction and perfect infallibility so long as we appreciate that this ideal is never instantiated, but such sentimentality must not be allowed to impede development of conceptual resources for mastering the panorama of partial certainties which are more literally relevant to the real world.
>
> (Rozeboom, 1967: 175–85)

McCloskey and Rozeboom are compelled to offer an alternative metaphysical "sentimental" world – albeit a thicker one – that for the reasons they so eloquently give will intervene in the "development of conceptual resources." This is a good illustration of what is so puzzling for metatheorists studying this old debate: Neither McCloskey nor Mäki are able to escape a certain paradigm which modern scientists find especially captivating. This deep-rooted concept is *synthesis*. Indeed even Derrida employs synthetic arguments, constructions, reconstructions, and other combinatory procedures, but he does not impose such a structure on the concept of knowledge and by implication truth.

The principal structural break between structuralism and post-structuralism appears to take place within the concept of the sign. However, by working with its double-science, deconstruction is able to reassert and even employ the mechanics of semiotics by displacing its differential foundation with a non-foundation of *différance*. Saussure's strict requirement for the sign to have a finite residue-free differential structure is the metaphysical core of his *Cours* (1907). Derrida recognizes the necessity of such a move if one seeks to distil a pure concept – functioning as a fixed fundamental reference that itself refers to nothing – from an infinite chain of intertextual relations that participate in the production of its meaning.

> Maintenance of the rigorous distinction – an essential and juridical distinction – between the *signans* [signifier-word] and the *signatum* [signified-concept] and the equation between *signatum* and the

concept leaves open in principle the possibility of conceiving of a *signified concept in itself*, a concept simply present to thought, independent from the linguistic system, that is to say from a system of signifiers. In leaving this possibility open, and it is so left by the very principle of the opposition between signifier and signified and thus of the sign, Saussure contradicts the critical acquisition of which we have spoken. He accedes to the traditional demand for what I have proposed to call a "transcendental signified," which in itself or in its essence would not refer to any signifier, which would transcend the chain of signs and at a certain moment would no longer itself function as a signifier. On the contrary, though, from the moment one puts in question the possibility of such a transcendental signifier, the distinction between signifier and signified and thus the notion of sign becomes problematic at its root.

(Derrida, 1972/1981: 29–30/19–20)

It is now commonplace to view the meaning-production process of signification as not a pair – arbitrary signifier and signified concept – but as a chain in which signified concepts function as signifiers for other concepts who, in turn, signify yet other signifieds, etc. Each link in such a chain is *contextually* determined as signifier or signified according to its function at a specific space–time location. This is what puts the *post-* in post-structuralism. However, the conceptual distinction between the *functions* of signifiers and signifieds is paramount to the study of language, and is necessary for any thought whatsoever. Deconstruction questions any foundational structure attributed to this distinction but, simultaneously, reaffirms and employs it to elucidate *the question of its necessity*. Jonathan Culler admonishes over-zealous post-structuralists of a potential and unfortunately common misunderstanding concerning what has sometimes been called (following Paul Feyerabend) "anything goes" or, more affectionately, "Derridadaism." I reproduce below in its entirety a passage I believe should be required reading for any aspiring critical theorist and postmodern philosopher:

However, literary critics should exercise caution in drawing inferences from this principle. While it does enjoin skepticism about possibilities of arresting meaning, or discovering a meaning that lies outside of and governs the play of signs in a text, it does not propose indeterminacy of meaning in the usual sense: the impossibility or unjustifiability of choosing one meaning over another. On the contrary, it is only because there may be excellent reasons for choosing one meaning rather than another that there is any point in insisting that the meaning chosen is itself also a signifier that can be interpreted in turn. The fact that any signified is also in the position of signifier does not mean that there are no reasons to link a signifier with one signified rather than another; still less does it suggest, as both hostile and sympathetic critics have claimed, an absolute priority of the signifier or a definition of the text as a galaxy of signifiers ... The structural redoubling of any signified as an interpretable signifier does suggest that the realm of signifiers acquires a certain autonomy, but this does not mean signifiers without signifieds, only the failure of signifieds to produce closure.

(Culler, 1982: 189)

McCloskey's reply to Mäki seems to end with a conciliatory paragraph that uses what speech-act theorist would perhaps call a performative of camaraderie. Such a performative would take the form: "you were nitpicking so I showed you that I can do the same to you; but after all we basically agree and respect each other, right comrade?" In McCloskey's words:

But I am emphasizing disagreements with Mäki, which in truth are minor. As I said, Mäki and I agree on a lot. We agree that economics has a rhetorical aspect, that sometimes its rhetoric is good and sometimes not so good. *Most of all I think we agree* that it's time to put away the philosophical tools, misunderstood and misused by most self-described philosophers of economics, and pick up the historical and sociological and rhetorical ones. There's more that such nonphilosophical tools can tell about what we're saying and how we're saying it. More, anyway, than the philosophers of 1955 shouting at us from their armchairs.

(McCloskey, 1995a: 1322, emphasis added)

The tone of camaraderie starts shifting after "Most of all I think we agree ..." and becomes rather shrill – from a *sprach*-ethical point of view – at the end. The performative must have been used ironically, to the effect of something more in line with a performative that I would name "maternal condescension." Maternal for its *passive*-aggressiveness of the smothering kind, and condescending for making such an obvious attack in a tone that suggests that the implied reader does not even appreciate the irony. On second thought, it is possible that this is a *demonstrative* move designed to show Mäki the aggression of his own performative of a more common kind in the diagnosis, which we could call "paternal condescension."

4 Proof

The rhetoric of truth

Modern epistemology against analytical philosophy[1]

At the very least, reading the Mäki–McCloskey conversation vividly high-lights the rhetoric dimension of the philosophy of economics and science in general. My implied reader is already aware of many of the postmodern complications that are in play within this polemic. Mäki's rhetoric is so haughtily sober and polite, while McCloskey's is so cynically playful and irreverent. Both authors insist on the similarity between them in such an overstressed manner that prompts me to consider the performative pur-poses and strategic designs emerging in their texts.

What is it that both McCloskey and Mäki agree upon? I would suggest the following as the only likely candidate: the recognition of the import-ance of rhetoric in the process of knowledge production, accumulation, and distribution. This is indeed not a minor agreement but – once they accept and promote it – they follow separate paths. John O'Neill (1998) and Ramón García Fernández (1999) suggest that the principal difference lies in the *role* of rhetoric:

> For the latter [Mäki], rhetoric would be compatible with, but not at the core of, economic knowledge, a position labeled "weak compati-bilism" between rhetoric and reason (or science, or philosophy). For the former [McCloskey], the relation between rhetoric and the pro-duction of knowledge would be more central, configuring a case of "strong compatibilism".
>
> (Fernández, 1999: n.p.)

Fernández also opines that Mäki's concern with the problem of truth is motivated in part by his reluctance to distance himself from mainstream economists – a political consideration. This is an interesting issue on which I have commented in my reading of McCloskey, and is very much alive in many open debates such as the one between Philip Mirowski and Antonio Callari over the concept of the gift and its relation to the structure of value in economics (see footnote 2 of Chapter 3, p. 128).

The issues of *naïveté* (angel theory of truth) and elitism (elite theory of truth) have been at the core of criticism raised against McCloskey. It is interesting to note how these criticisms take a tone reflective of the political arena: Left-leaning critics stress the weaknesses of her "liberal" (English definition) elitist criterion for truth, while right-leaning ones stress the weaknesses of her "liberal" (American definition) *sprachethik* idealist criterion for truth. McCloskey is paying a toll for employing a *non-monist* (multiple) process of inquiry. Like a mythical troll guarding a bridge, the archive charges an analytical tariff for the production of knowledge that is structured non-paradigmatically. McCloskey's economic criticism has this too in common with deconstruction: It is structurally alien to any synthetic school of thought. In opposition to Mäki, *my* suggestion for McCloskey is to cut the awkward apologetic ties that hold back her analysis and be more like deconstruction because only a meticulous and at times disturbing reevaluation of the archive could ever penetrate the obscurity of language.

For example, consider the criticism regarding her naive reliance on *sprachethik* for establishing small-t truths in economics. The problem here is her uncritical humanistic belief in the satisfactorily functioning of democracy *and* of markets. This is why she alienated many of her most sympathetic readers who cannot accept that the mere insertion of virtuous institutions such as democracy and markets into the archive's adjudicative process guarantees virtuous science.

The double-gesture of deconstruction has been an important influence on McCloskey via its paramount influence on literary theory. At the heart of deconstruction lies the double-procedure for deconstructing hierarchical oppositions, which I present schematically (and highly reductively) here:

1   Show opposition is metaphysical (ideological) by revealing its presuppositions and its function in the metaphysical system it supports. Seen as a strategic function, the opposition auto-deconstructs the texts that employ it.
2   Simultaneously maintain the opposition by employing it in your own argument, but with its hierarchy reversed. The strategic functions of the rhetoric of hierarchical oppositions are revealed through the effects of this reversal, along with their role in the texts that employ them and the metaphysical system they support.

Consider as an illustration the position of deconstruction (or any other offshoot such as McCloskey's rhetoric or Tony Lawson's critical realism) in the *politics* of knowledge. In Jonathan Culler's words:

> [Such a position] can always be attacked both as an *anarchism* determined to disrupt any order whatever and, from the opposite perspect-

ive, as an *accessory* to the hierarchies it denounces. Instead of claiming to offer firm ground for the construction of a new order or synthesis, it remains implicated in or attached to the system it criticizes and attempts to displace.

(Culler, 1982: 150, emphasis added)

This damned-if-you-do-and-damned-if-you-don't position in which what could be termed post-synthetic inquiry finds itself vis-à-vis the dominant synthetic approaches brings us back to epistemology which is – as McCloskey's reply correctly claims – the major difference between our two protagonists and indeed the first item on the agenda of current philosophy of all flavors.

Jonathan Culler defines reality as "the presence behind representations, what accurate representations are representations of" and philosophy as "a theory of representation" (Culler, 1982: 152). This should illuminate the philosopher of science Richard Rorty's discussion of epistemology's role within philosophy in his famous *Philosophy and the Mirror of Nature*:

Philosophy as a discipline thus sees itself as the attempt to underwrite or debunk claims to knowledge made by science, morality, art or religion. It purports to do this on the basis of its special understanding of the nature of knowledge and of mind. Philosophy can be foundational in respect to the rest of culture because culture is the assemblage of claims to knowledge, and philosophy adjudicates such claims. It can do so because it understands the foundations of knowledge and it finds these foundations in a study of man-as-knower, of the "mental processes" or the "activity of representation" which make knowledge possible. To know is to represent accurately what is outside the mind; so to understand the possibility and nature of knowledge is to understand the way in which the mind is able to construct such representations.

(Rorty, 1980: 3)

Pragmatists such as McCloskey call to doubt not only the truth of our present beliefs but the criteria for truthful inquiry. This is why they have been, and still are, problematic for philosophy as a discipline. The pragmatic solution is to discard the basic definition of truth as what *is*, in favor of viewing truth as dependent on a system of justification. Pragmatists can thus consider themselves as realists, providing that truth be defined as a McCloskian small-t truth: Anything goes … so long as enough prominent academics agree. A Derridian deconstructive perspective cannot allow the acceptance of the hierarchical opposition in the pragmatic truth, which is founded on the *norm* that is, by definition, a product of the exclusion of the non-normal. In this, I find myself in the analytical camp with Mäki. Deconstruction explicitly reaffirms the role of epistemology as underwriting theory and especially its self-reflexive character. Though epistemology cannot, as pragmatists assert, supply us with foundations on which to build new theories, it should not be rejected since it foregrounds the evolution of assumptions, institutions, and practices.

The Mäki–McCloskey debate highlights some of the problems associated with the distinction between reading and understanding and misreading and misunderstanding as they relate to rational reconstructions as such. The difference is usually perceived as that between preserving and reproducing meaning, and distorting and introducing differences. What is the characteristic of a text that allows it to be at least potentially understood by different people in different contexts? Derrida shows that the most general definition of writing is often based on the notion of *iterability*. Even in its simplest role as a means to convey a speaker's words to a third party, writing must be repeatable in the sense that the signifiers must function repeatedly while separated from any original speaker. However, this will hold for signs in general which must be recognized as such in different circumstances in order to function.

> If "writing" means inscription and especially the durable instituting of signs (and this is the only irreducible kernel of the concept of writing), then writing in general covers the entire domain of linguistic signs … The very idea of institution, hence of the arbitrariness of the sign, is unthinkable prior to or outside the horizon of writing.
>
> (Derrida, 1976: 44)

All the iterations that a text generates involve some degree of modification, some of which will achieve the status of "understood" if the differences they introduced are deemed sufficiently insignificant. The reversal is now complete: Understanding is a special case of misunderstanding; it is misunderstanding whose misses do not matter. I have preserved here the distinction between misunderstandings that matter and those that do not while exposing the metaphysics of preserving authorial intent as a system of value judgments – the double gesture at work. Now we are able to see the history of thought, reading, and writing as a history of misunderstanding, misreading, and miswriting some of which have under certain circumstances been regarded as understanding, reading, and writing. This approach is attuned to the interpretative relations supporting any narrative in the history of thought, while stressing the contextual and indeed ephemeral nature of knowledge-claims. The postmodern critic Barbara Johnson writes (or miswrites):

> The sentence "all readings are misreadings" does not *simply* deny the notion of truth. Truth is preserved in vestigial form in the notion of error. This does not mean that there is, somewhere out there, forever unattainable, the one true reading against which all others will be tried

and found wanting. Rather, it implies 1) that the reasons a reading might consider itself *right* are motivated and undercut by its own interests, blindness, desires, and fatigue, and 2) that the *role* of truth cannot be so easily eliminated. Even if truth is but a fantasy of the will to power, *something* still marks the point from which the imperatives of the not-self make themselves felt.

(Johnson, 1980: 14)

I have looked at the Mäki–McCloskey debate in some detail because I take it to be a particularly relevant illustration of the epistemological incommensurability that lurks in most methodological debates in economics today. Mäki's position – sometimes referred to as "idealization-abstraction" – is itself particularly instrumental for my purposes because he is explicitly addressing rhetorical issues arising within the meta-theory of economics. He is also one of the few economic philosophers who directly and explicitly engaged McCloskey's work, and attempted to bridge the epistemological gap with what he had at least hoped would be an internal criticism. It turns out that the polite performatives of camaraderie in which both McCloskey and Mäki have indulged throughout their debate may have been less cynical than I initially suspected. They *do* agree on almost everything except for their epistemological framework, which is probably the most intractable of all essentially contested concepts.

The production of knowledge

It is now finally time to introduce Foucauldian analysis explicitly. One quickly discovers that a Derridian epistemological reading, like *micro-economic* theory, is very capable in examining a specific rhetoric phenomenon within a well-defined context, but is insufficient for broad historical studies in which the dynamics of contexts are a major issue. Michel Foucault's ideas have already been recognized as paramount to contemporary history, sociology, anthropology, science studies, and literary criticism, and many Foucauldian principles have even established themselves – albeit mostly via the back door – in the study of the history of economic thought and the philosophy of economics. My first task is to reconstruct a Foucauldian epistemology from the vast body of work in which it lies hidden. Foucault is much more accepted, studied, and referenced than Derrida due to what I believe is a false sense of accessibility his works provide. Much like McCloskey, he produces very convincing and readable texts that rely heavily on empirical data. The difficulty in Foucault is that he draws few general philosophical conclusions *within* the texts, and thus forces critics to work through all the archeological metaphors (*The Archaeology of Knowledge*, 1969/1972), mental asylums (*The Birth of the Clinic*, 1972/1973), and medieval dungeons (*Discipline and Punish*, 1975/1977), in which threads of the Foucauldian philosophy are to be found.

Foucault directed his attention to the sustaining relationships between truth, power, and discourse. His description of these relationships often sounds a lot like economics or, more precisely, political economics:

> There can be no possible exercise of power without a certain economy of discourses of truth which operates through and on the basis of this association. We are subjected to the production of truth through power and we cannot exercise power except through the production of truth. This is the case of every society, but I believe that in ours the relationship between power, right, and truth is organized in a highly specific fashion ... I would say that we are forced to produce the truth of power that our society demands, of which it has need, in order to function we must speak the truth; we are constrained or condemned to confess to or discover the truth. Power never ceases its interrogation, its inquisition, its registration of truth; it institutionalizes, professionalizes and rewards its pursuit. In the last analysis, we must produce truth as we must produce wealth.
>
> (Foucault, 1976a: 93)

Foucault constructs a framework with which to examine the workings of the "economy of discourses of truth" in *The Archaeology of Knowledge* (1969), building on economic and anthropological concepts.

Foucault's close friend and eminent philosopher Gilles Deleuze uses the familiar concept of scarcity to argue that statements are scarce because "one phrase denies the existence of others, forbidding, contradicting or repressing them to such an extent that each phrase remains pregnant with everything left unsaid" (Deleuze, 1986: 2). Phrases and propositions multiply via a process of contradiction and abstraction that is theory. The "brute facts" of this process are statements for which contradiction and abstraction are possible but *arbitrary*. The structure emerges from the *regularities* in the statements (what Derrida calls their iterability), since in order to be repeatable and comprehensible in different contexts, statements must be changeable.

Foucault's concept of discourse can be seen as a family of statements that are subjected to a set of ideological rules, conventions, and customs. In the words of the critic Roger Fowler:

> "Discourse" is speech or writing seen from the point of view of the beliefs, values and categories which it embodies; these beliefs (etc.) constitute a way of looking at the world, an organization or representation of experience – "ideology" in the neutral, non-pejorative sense. Different modes of discourse encode different representations of experience; and the source of these representations is the communicative context within which discourse is embedded.
>
> (Fowler, 1990, in Hawthorn, 1992: 48)

Foucault uses his study of power relations in *Discipline and Punish: The Birth of the Prison* (1975/1977) to extend the Marxist tradition by interpreting it in an innovative way. He employs a functionalist approach: Power is not a property but a strategy, not an attribute but a relation. "[P]ower is not homogeneous but can be defined only by the particular points through which it passes" (Deleuze, 1986: 25). The trappings of power – the state for example – are the effect of the structure of power operating at a different level. Power resides in the tension between institutions and classes; it does not *originate* in institutions and classes. "Relations of power are not in a position of exteriority with respect to other types of relationships ... they have a directly productive role, wherever they come into play" (Foucault, 1976b: 124, in Deleuze, 1986: 27, endnote 4).

This concept of power is lacking in any source or origin, and operates on two distinct forms: the visible (content), and things that can be articulated (expression). These formations relate to each other via mutual presupposition – coherence – not via any sort of direct correspondence (see the *Division* above). Form can have two meanings: organizing matter (a journal article for example), or organizing functions (the process and concept of peer-review for example). The notion that knowledge is gained by *suspending* power relations – McCloskey's *herrschaftsfrei* (dominance-free) *sprachethik* for example – is thus misguided. Knowledge is produced by making specific connections between the visible and the "articulable." It thus refers to and acts via some sort of power, which in turn relies on knowledge for its processes of differentiation. In *Discipline and Punish*, Foucault maintains that "there is no power relation without the correlative constitution of a field of knowledge that does not presuppose and constitute at the same time power relations" (Foucault, 1975/1977: 32/27).

Foucault espouses a thoroughly historical and textualist view according to which "An 'age' does not pre-exist the statements which express it, nor the visibilities which fill it" (Deleuze, 1986: 48). In the positivist age, for example, peer-reviewed journal articles (non-discursive/visible) became a primary form of seeing and displaying cognitively significant (non-metaphysical) economics. Throughout their history, disciplines produce a system of statements concerning the concept of scientific legitimacy (verifiability, falsification, etc.). It is important to note that the primacy of statements does not imply in any way that the non-discursive can be reduced to statements. The realization that texts are to be found everywhere relating to everything calls for an enlargement of the concept of text, *not* for the reduction of the universe to prose. This point cannot, I believe, be overstressed.

There is no isomorphism between the visible and the articulable and the relations between determination and the determinable element are non-relations. Foucault illustrates this with René Magritte's *The Treachery of Images* (1929), which features a pipe suspended in mid air above the words: *Ceci n'est pas une pipe* (*This is not a pipe*). The surrealistic point Magritte is making is about the complex interdependency of context and frame. In our context here, the constative statement taken *within* the frame of the picture would seem to be false – it *is* a painting of a pipe after all. However it is a *painting* of a pipe, not a pipe. In other words, if we allow the *outside* of the frame to contaminate the *inside*, then the statement is true – this is a painting *not* a pipe. Neither the painting nor the statement is actually a pipe and thus the ironically false statement: *This is not a pipe* is in fact a true statement. The falseness of the statement can only be established within the context of a pictureframe which presupposes the position of looking at a painting. It is thus that we *determine* a painting of a pipe – purely symbolic with no painted context within the frame – as a true representation of a pipe. Magritte introduces the ironic false statement as an uncanny repetition of the repressed knowledge that *in accepting the truth of art, we are in fact worshiping idols.*

The view that "truth is inseparable from the procedure establishing it" (Deleuze, 1986: 63), is the basis for Deleuze's reading of Foucauldian philosophy as pragmatic. In *Discipline and Punish* (1975/1977), Foucault compares models of science in different ages: the "inquisitorial inquiry" of the late middle age, and the "disciplinary examination" of the late eighteenth century. The procedure is always made of a *process*, which is a mechanical visibility, and a *method*, which is a statement. The mechanics of being burned at the stake are determined by the statements to the effect that a criminal has performed a crime against the Church, which will, in turn, exact its justifiable revenge. The mechanics of being diagnosed as suffering from Attention Deficit Hyperactivity Disorder, being relegated to euphemistically labeled special education schooling, and being prescribed Ritalin, are determined by the statements to the effect that a child displays levels of activity in excess of those deemed appropriate for a specifically structured schooling system. The philosophical implications of this exhaustive dismal history is that truth is accessible to knowledge only via multiple problematizations, and that a history of truth is a practice constituted by a process and a method – two forms that are engaged in a problematic non-relation between the visible and the articulable. Paraphrasing Deleuze: what we see never lies in what we say, and what we say never lies in what we see.

According to Deleuze, the many patched-up versions of realism (correspondence, correlative, conjunctional, critical, transcendental, etc.) are non-solutions for Foucault because

> the statement has its own correlative object and is not a proposition designating a state of things or a visible object. As logic would have it; but neither is the visible a mute meaning, a signified of power to be realized in language, as phenomenology would have it. The archive, the audiovisual is disjunctive.
>
> (Deleuze, 1986: 64)

The irreducible duplicity of knowledge or this disjunctive gap within the archive between specific visibilities and systematic statements is maintained by a relation between forces who, in turn, are also power relations existing in relation to other forces. Deleuze points out that this is not a return to natural law philosophy because law is a form of expression and nature is a form of visibility while Foucault's forces have only each other as both object and subject (Deleuze, 1986: 70). Power relations are thus actions upon actions (to induce, assume, enlarge, reduce, and constrain, for example). The relation between power (itself constituted by relations between forces) and knowledge (historical formations or *strata* constituted by the relations between forms) is not unlike the economic concepts of flows and stocks: Power relations are non-stratified strategies that flow through particular local and unstable points of tension. Knowledge, on the other hand, is stratified and archived through the formal conditions of seeing and speaking. The instability of the flow of power means that power cannot be completely known because the practice of power is irreducible to any particular practice of knowledge. The form of knowledge (*connaissance*, Methods – with a capital M for McCloskey) is constrained by a "diagram" of power relations that is itself constrained by forces of practical knowledge (*savoirs*, processes) which actualize it.

> Between techniques of knowledge and strategies of power, there is no exteriority, even if they have their specific roles and are linked together on the basis of their difference.
>
> (Foucault, 1976/1984: 130/98)

Actualization stratifies power relations by *locally* integrating specific features or visible characteristics of power. There is a multiplicity of local and/or partial integrations tracing specific relations or particular points. Institutions are such integrations: They have no interiority and are practices that rather than explain power, pre-suppose its relations. "There is no State, only state control" (Deleuze, 1986: 75). So to understand knowledge – the stated object of epistemology – one must examine each institution in each historical formation in terms of the power relations it integrates, its relations with other institutions, and the way in which all the above changes from stratum to stratum. The integrations/institutions themselves are also multiplicities consisting of visible apparatuses such as the police, and articulable rules such as the penal code.

There is a controversy surrounding Foucault over the question of whether there is a primacy of power over knowledge. This is perhaps a similar political controversy to that surrounding Niccolò Machiavelli's investigation of the relationship between institutions and power. Like a prince without his subjects, knowledge would be a function without an argument if there were no differential power relations to integrate. The power diagram is nevertheless dependent on knowledge for its actualization and would therefore remain mute in its absence. This is mutual presupposition: relations of knowledge presuppose, and are implied by, relations of power:

> If power is not simply violence, this is not only because it passes in itself through categories that express the relation between two forces but also because, in relation to knowledge, it produces truth, in so far as it makes us see and speak.
>
> (Deleuze, 1986: 83, endnote 18)

Universal concepts such as human rights are no more than massive effects due to a specific distribution of particular features in a particular stratum under a particular process of formalization. The only case in which the universal is co-nescient with the statement is mathematics. This view could at least partly explain the privileged position mathematics holds in relation to its perceived truth-content. Even though – and perhaps precisely because – mathematics operates in a realm that is perhaps the most removed from the real world, it is perceived by modern society as having a privileged access to it.

Foucault's major achievement according to Deleuze is the conversion of phenomenology into epistemology:

> For seeing and speaking means knowing [*savoir*], but we do not see what we speak about, nor do we speak about what we see; and when we see a pipe we shall always say (in one way or another): "this is not a pipe", as though intentionality denied itself, and collapsed into itself. Everything is knowledge, and that is the first reason why there is no "savage experience": there is nothing beneath or prior to knowledge. But knowledge is irreducibly double, since it involves speaking and seeing, language and light, which is the reason why there is no intentionality.
>
> (Deleuze, 1986: 109)

Prior to phenomenology, intentionality was seen as the relation between consciousness and its object. This line of thought is sometimes called *psychologism* and has its roots in the naturalist tradition. Phenomenologists such as Martin Heidegger and Maurice Merleau-Ponty already substituted intentionality with ontology and Foucault takes the extra step from ontology to epistemology via the doubling of *being* into language-being (murmur) and light-being (shimmer) which refer to statements and visibilities respectively. Any subject–object intentionality cannot bridge the gap between the two parts that constitute knowledge: From the psyche via being to knowledge. If there is a struggle to maintain or reinstate intentionality – including an insistence on possible access to objective reality – then it operates at the level of the power diagram which is the only level that flows *between* the murmur and the shimmer – the a priori of statements and visibilities. In the Kantian philosopher Sir W. Hamilton's words, the a priori are

> those elements of knowledge which are not obtained *a posteriori*; are not evolved out of experience as facticious generalizations; but which, as native to, are potentially in, the mind antecedent to the act of experience.
>
> (Hamilton, 1841: 762/1, in the Oxford English Dictionary under
> "a priori," entry number 3)

The archeology of knowledge deals with three historical and ontological dimensions: knowledge, power, and self. "Knowledge-being" is determined by specific forms assumed at any moment by the visible and the articulable because light and language are determined in a given historical formation. "Power-being" is determined by relations between forces that vary between different ages. "Self-being," is determined by the process of subjectivation or self-presence, which depends on what Derrida calls "hearing/understanding oneself speak" (see *What is deconstruction* in the *Narration*, page 30). Our relationship with the march of time and history itself – what I would call "time-being" to cohere with Foucault's terminology – is particularly problematic. For Kant, the relation to oneself is memory that is generated by a process of subjectivation. For Foucault, time moves across strata in the same way as it does in a geological cross-section. Deleuze links this approach to Nietzsche:

> On the limit of the strata, the whole of the inside finds itself actively present on the outside. The inside condenses the past (a long period of time) in ways that are not at all continuous but instead confront it with a future that comes from outside, exchange it and re-create it. To think means to be embedded in the present-time stratum that serves as a limit: what can I see and what can I say today? But this involves thinking of the past as it is condensed in the inside, in the relation to oneself (there is a Greek in me, or a Christian, and so on). We will then think the past against the present and resist the latter, not in favour of a return but "in favour, I hope, of a time to come."
>
> (Nietzsche in Deleuze, 1986: 119)

The new realists: critical and transcendental

In this section, I will briefly outline several different positions from which criticism has been raised against McCloskey and the rhetorical position. Due to terminological conflicts and complications in the literature that I will present here, it is important to clarify that most recent commentators have identified McCloskey's philosophical position as ostensibly postmodern.

McCloskey's postmodernism in my view is primarily characterized by her deconstructionist epistemological duality or even multiplicity, but it should be clear by now that this moniker is highly ambiguous and can be interpreted in a multitude of different and often conflicting ways. Be that as it may (and apart from the diligent Mäki), most criticisms against McCloskey have been framed within criticisms against postmodern philosophy of science.

One of the most influential recent books in the meta-theory of economics is Tony Lawson's *Economics and Reality* (1997). This book is the culmination of several papers in which he applies the work of the Cambridge philosopher Roy Bhaskar in an attempt to develop a sustainable realist position for the philosophy of economics. Bhaskar's "transcendental realism," first expressed in his *A Realist Theory of Science* (Bhaskar, 1975), is derived from Kant's designation for the opponents of his "transcendental idealism" as it is most explicitly developed in the *Critique of Pure Reason* (1787). For Kant, transcendental realism was the position of those who view "time and space as something given in themselves, independently of our sensibility" (Kant, 1787: 346). The Kantian mind affects itself in the form of time (subjective memory) while it is affected by other things in the form of space.

Bhaskar had initially coined two terms to describe his work:

> I had initially called my general philosophy of science "transcendental realism" and my special philosophy of the human sciences "critical naturalism". Gradually people started to elide the two and refer to the hybrid as "critical realism". It struck me that there were good reasons not to demur at the mongrel. For a start, Kant had styled his transcendental idealism the "critical philosophy". Transcendental realism had as much right to the title of critical realism.
>
> (Bhaskar, 1989: 190)

It is indeed by far more common to encounter the term "critical realism" than "transcendental realism" though Lawson (1997) attempts to revert to the original distinction. He however introduces another semantic ambiguity by using the term "critical realism" to refer to a specific philosophy of the human sciences – what Bhaskar calls "critical naturalism." In my opinion, this is unfortunate since while "critical naturalism" captures the idea of placing limits on the applicability of scientific method to the social sciences, "critical realism" is devoid of any such signification. Furthermore, as argued by the leading critical realist Andrew Collier (1994: xi), the term "critical" is inappropriate for a philosophical *position* because it is a term of approval in contrast with "dogmatic" or "naive."

Transcendental realism was developed explicitly as a critique of positivism. Its aim was to solve some of the fundamental problems encountered by the growth-of-knowledge theorists. In Bhaskar's words:

A problem of all these trends [specifically Popperians, Kuhnians, and Wittgensteinians] was to sustain a clear concept of the continued independent *reality* of *being* – of the intransitive or ontological dimension – in the face of the *relativity* of our *Knowledge* – in the transitive or epistemological dimension.

(Bhaskar, 1998: x)

The problem of incommensurability between theories seems to lead to relativist skepticism about the existence of a theory-independent world, or at least about any possibility for rational theory-choice. Bhaskar's (1975: 248) solution is to note that theories relate to each other not only by difference but also by *conflict*. This presupposes that they share a worldly battleground that is perhaps not the real world in the sense of being perception-independent, but at least a compatible account of the world. This allows Bhaskar to reinstate the possibility and validity of internal methodological criticism along similar lines as proposed by Caldwell and others:

[I]f one theory can explain more significant phenomena in terms of its descriptions than the other can in terms of *its*, then there is a rational criterion for theory choice, and *a fortiori* a positive sense to the idea of scientific development over time.

(Bhaskar, 1998: xi)

Transcendental realism offers an alternative for the positivist hypothetical-deductive model of explanation, which links testable hypotheses with higher-order hypotheses, theories, and eventually universal laws. Universal laws are identified through the process of experimentation, which, by definition, limits the actual universality (theoretical or empirical) of said laws, by the specificity and necessity of the experimental framework.

Laws, then, and the workings of nature have to be analyzed dispositionally as the powers, or more precisely tendencies, or underlying generative mechanisms which may on the one hand – the horizontal aspect – be possessed unexercised, exercised unactualized, and actualized undetected or unperceived; and on the other – the vertical aspect – be discovered in an ongoing irreducibly empirical open-ended process of scientific development. A transcendental argument from the conditions of the possibility of experimentation in science thus establishes at once the irreducibility of ontology, of the theory of being, to epistemology and a novel non-empiricist but non-rationalist, non-actualist, stratified and differentiated ontology, that is characterized by the prevalence of structures as well as events (stratification) and open systems as well as closed (differentiation).

(Bhaskar, 1998: xii)

The reader will immediately recognize the structure and vocabulary of Michel Foucault (see *The Production of Knowledge* above and Foucault, 1966b/1970) whom Bhaskar lists in his bibliography, but does not engage to any extent commensurable with the similarities of their respective ideas. Indeed I find that the literature of Critical Realism is woefully lacking in explicit Foucauldian references. Given the broad epistemological and onto-logical similarities, which any reader familiar with the two literatures will immediately detect, I would (hesitantly) venture to opine that the implied historiography of critical realism is genealogically misleading. It may be that the relatively incestuous body of works in critical realism – almost exclusively Cambridge philosophers (see for example the papers in Archer and all, 1998) – deprived us of a fruitfully reflexive explicit debate on such a potentially powerful application of Foucauldian sociology to the problems of the philosophy of science. The scope of this text cannot accommodate an adequate presentation of Lawson's application of transcendental realism to economic philosophy. I will therefore concentrate solely on the specific issues he raises with regard to McCloskey and his more general critique of the postmodern approaches to economic philosophy.

Anti-methodology

Lawson addresses the meta-methodological issues underlying his project in a chapter aptly titled "The Nature of the Argument." His only direct criti-cism of McCloskey comes in the context of the debate over the usefulness and indeed possibility of prescriptive methodology. Lawson reconstructs the anti-methodological position from fragments of texts by McCloskey, Philip Mirowski, Roy Weintraub, and even Bruce Caldwell. The inclusion of Caldwell is particularly puzzling since he specifically asserts a quasi-prescriptive role for methodology in rationally reconstructing, comparing, and internally criticizing different meta-theoretical positions – this is hardly an anti-methodological position. I have already discussed many of the problems associated with prescriptive methodology but Lawson's argument is specifically directed to an aggregated position that can be neatly summar-ized with a notorious phrase from Roy Weintraub's "Methodology Doesn't Matter, But the History of Thought Might":

> [A]ny normative role for Methodology rests upon a profound miscon-ception [foundationalism: a privileged outside position], and thus Methodology cannot possibly have consequences for the way eco-nomics is done. Methodology ... cannot have any impact on the manner of practice.
> (Weintraub, 1989: 478, in Lawson, 1997: 295–6, footnote 2)

The special mode of inquiry that crosses the threshold of "scientificity" by virtue of complying with a prescriptive methodology has been repeatedly problematized in the literature and in this text. There is however an important basis for this prescriptive skepticism that Lawson fails to discuss. I am referring to the evolutionary descriptive basis elaborated by Feyerabend in *Against Method* (1975) and Kuhn's *Structure* (1962) (see Balak, 2000). Feyerabend's argument – which is yet to deploy its full ordinance on the philosophy of science – was essentially that science has never followed an a priori methodology and thus any progress we are willing to admit (teleological, as positivist would have it, or not, as critical realists would have it) could not have been the result of following a prescriptive methodology.

Notwithstanding the significant contribution Lawson has made in introducing, systematizing, and applying an interesting post-positivist philosophical position to the economic profession, like many others he has failed to seriously accost some of the most enduring problems in the philosophy of the social sciences. In accusing even Caldwell of an overly hesitant position with regard to methodological prescription, and disparaging the growing concern with (and subsequent literature on) the tensions between methodology and *practice* in economics, he has undermined the most interesting and potentially fruitful link in his own work. This link is in the realm of the history of thought (Weintraub would approve) and is precisely the postmodern tradition that has informed "the writings of McCloskey, Mirowski and Weintraub along with most others who engage in meta-methodology" (Lawson, 1997: 298, note 13). Lawson thus finds an explicit postmodern position in the ideas of his fellow post-positivists in economics on top of the implicit yet unacknowledged postmodern basis for his *own* ideas. He only sees fit to enlighten us as to the workings of these ideas in the few pages he dedicates to McCloskey, Mirowski, and Weintraub, and directs us to yet another Cambridge economist (his graduate student) in the last words of an endnote: "On all this see Sofianou, 1995" (Lawson, 1997: 295, note 1). He is referring to a paper by Evanthia Sofianou titled "Post-modernism and the Notion of Rationality in Economics" in – you guessed it – the *Cambridge Journal of Economics*. I will look at this paper in the next section.

The "straw-woman" of postmodernism

Sofianou's (1995) is an interesting paper that touches on many issues regarding postmodern approaches to modeling economic behavior in contrast to the familiar orthodox behaviorist models. Her philosophical position is squarely within the emerging literature of critical realism and she is evaluating postmodernism's effectiveness as an ally against positivism and not so much as an alternative position to her own. The relevance of this paper for my purposes is to illustrate the ambiguous rhetorical niche which the term postmodernism occupies in much of the current philosophical literature in economics and to point to some of the ways in which it is misunderstood. It is in this sense that I use the term "straw-woman" as a "politically correct" caricature of the naive and reduced reconstruction of postmodernism in most of the antagonistic literature and even, as is the case here, in relatively complementary positioned texts.

I will use Sofianou's own abstract to describe the paper:

> The article assesses contributions from economists who see the post-modernist framework as providing a viable alternative to the behaviouristic model of action in economics. It is found that although post-modernism identifies many of the problems of mainstream economics it too remains unable to sustain the notions of choice and agency which it preaches because it fails to escape the anthropocentrism of positivist philosophy. Once this anthropocentrism is abandoned, it can be seen that agency lies not only in linguistic redescription but also in the understanding of real causal mechanisms which exist and act independently of any human agents.
>
> (Sofianou, 1995: 373)

The conclusions she draws are based on showing how postmodernism is unable to escape auto-deconstruction, an inability that, as we have seen, is shared by all systematic knowledge, and is at any rate more of an indicator of argumentative strength than of analytical weakness. Derridian deconstruction stands out with regard to its attitude towards auto-deconstruction in that instead of denying, hiding, or resisting it, deconstruction *celebrates* it.

Specifically, she reconstructs the important postmodern rejection of the subject–object distinction as a move from the positivistic view of the world as *our* knowledge about it, to the postmodern view of the world as *our* language about it (Sofianou, 1995: 377). It is in this sense that she accuses postmodernism of subscribing to a positivistic anthropocentrism.

> The general conclusion is that it [postmodernism] goes too far in its linguistification of reality in remaining narrowly anthropocentric, and in so doing renders both the possibility of knowledge, hence criticism and critique, unsustainable, and with it, agency and choice based on knowledge an impossibility ... [P]ost-modernism recognises the mistakes embedded in foundationalist positivism, only to end up dismissing the possibility of (fallible) knowledge. In so doing, it neglects the indispensability of structure for the enactment of human agency and therefore is unable to see that knowledge of this structure is a prerequisite for the enactment of agency.
>
> (Sofianou, 1995: 387)

It should be pointed out that this argument is quite similar to the one forwarded by Lawson in his critique of what I called above the anti-methodological position. The levels of inquiry are however different: Sofi-anou is attempting to restore human agency at the level of economic science while Lawson employs the same argument in restoring the role of prescriptive methodology at the meta-theoretical level.

This depiction is furthermore entirely untrue with regard to Derridian deconstruction. As should be clear by now, Derridian postmodernism does not even attempt to replace positivist foundations but to study their working. In this sense, it has sometimes been designated a higher level of inquiry labeled meta-meta-theory (!). The point is that contextual know-ledge is quite possible, and this possibility is based on the possibility of human agency to structurally repeat itself in recognizable and meaningful forms. Foucauldian sociology is already very similar to Bhaskarian and Lawsonian critical realism. What its proponents are missing is that the Kantian essentialism (the transcendental element) that is the linchpin of Lawson's prescriptive methodology as applied to economics, could use a healthy dose of Derridian "linguistification." Foucault and Derrida's work (and others like McCloskey working in this tradition) on how meaning is locally and temporally stratified, packaged, and communi-cated, needs to be incorporated into a critical realist approach in order for the latter to constitute a viable and significant step beyond methodo-logical pluralism.

Roger Backhouse, who is overall less than thrilled with the prospects of Lawson's Critical Realism, is a much more astute reader of post-modernism. In *Truth and Progress in Economic Knowledge*, he summar-izes the postmodern position in methodology as follows:

> [K]nowledge is the property of specific communities and ... it has to be understood as context-dependent. The absence of any knowledge that is not the property of a specific community is then taken to imply that there can be no objective, absolute knowledge that transcends discourse communities.
>
> ...
>
> This argument that the absence of any privileged source of knowledge undermines the idea of methodology rests on a specific view of what philosophy is. Philosophy, the argument runs, is assumed to offer insights into the nature of knowledge in general, which are then used to pass judgment on knowledge claims in particular fields ... Given that philosophy is simply one discourse amongst others, this view is, its critics argue, simply unsustainable.
>
> (Backhouse, 1997: 42)

While highly reductive, these paragraphs are a fair description of the post-modern anti-methodological position. There is however an important element missing in Backhouse's definition when he fails to explicitly recog-nize the non-synthetic structure of sophisticated postmodern argumentation.

While the hegemony of traditional philosophy is indeed undone, no other dialectic system is inserted in its place; no synthesis is attempted. Much is achieved by "merely" elucidating the underlying structures and strategies with which philosophy, prescriptive methodology, and the whole institutional edifice of rationality have been producing, and continue to produce, our knowledge of the world.

Backhouse also produces a brief survey of the criticism that has been forwarded against the postmodern position in economics. He argues on what he calls "more practical reasons" (Backhouse, 1997: 44, note 1), that postmodernism can be conservative because, by rejecting all but internal standards, it sustains the status quo. This coheres with Mäki's diagnosis of McCloskey in which he views her definition of truth as elitist since it relies on a consensus among academic elites (see *Division*, page 49). It is an endogenous complaint deriving from postmodernism's structural characteristics. As I argued in the previous section, the post-synthetic structural characteristic of the postmodern positions often leads to it being accused of being conservative in a radical guise because, as Jonathan Culler explains: "[i]nstead of claiming to offer firm ground for the construction of a new order or synthesis, it remains implicated in or attached to the system it criticizes and attempts to displace" (Culler, 1982: 150). Backhouse illustrates this with McCloskey's "Chicago School" assumption that "[t]here is no need for philosophical lawmaking or methodological regulation to keep the economy of the intellect running just fine" (McCloskey, 1986, in Backhouse, 1997: 32). Backhouse also maintains that beyond its potential conservatism, the "elite theory of truth" (to use Mäki's terminology, which I labeled *realpolitik* truth) cannot justifiably function as a justification for knowledge claims. This is because it is a logical tautology in which "the definition of the community determines knowledge" (Backhouse, 1997: 46). Furthermore, as observed by Hutchison (1992), the value of a product should be determined by the consumers of that activity, not the producers. I'm not quite sure however how to interpret this idea since it would seem to me that knowledge is an intermediary good, and is both consumed and produced by a discourse community composed of the same people. This would then suggest that the discourse community involved in these debates should look at Piero Sraffa's *Production of Commodities by Means of Commodities: Prelude to a Critique of Political Economy* (1960) which deals with particularities of intermediary production and calls for significant adjustments to the economic theories of production and industrial organization.

Another question concerns the impact of the postmodern epistemological skepticism on the actual practice of economics. Backhouse claims that "postmodernist arguments end up treating all knowledge as similar in kind, whereas in practice this is not the case" (Backhouse, 1997: 45). In practice, in a certain context it is possible to produce historically stratified empirical evidence that could then be a basis for the production of certain kinds of knowledge. Neither Foucault nor Derrida nor McCloskey nor I would have any objection to this claim. Furthermore, Backhouse continues to meta-prescribe a mode of prescriptive methodology that corresponds quite well to the kind of *sprachethik* McCloskey herself prescribes for methodology with a lowercase-m:

> We could then use our knowledge of contemporary economics and the history of economic thought, together with such ideas from philosophy or any other relevant discipline, to explore the nature of economic knowledge and to make such generalizations as we can concerning the way in which economic knowledge progresses. Though the results of such inquiries will always remain, to a greater or lesser extent, conjectural, there is no reason in principle why they should not be used as the basis for methodological prescriptions. Such prescriptions will, inevitably, be only as strong as the arguments on which they are based, but that is no reason why they should not be made and debated.
>
> (Backhouse, 1997: 45)

This passage would in fact seem to be more of a defense of postmodernism than a critique. Backhouse concludes that "discourse analysis (whether we see this as literary criticism, sociology of scientific knowledge, rhetorical analysis or whatever) and methodology are *complements*, not substitutes" (Backhouse, 1997: 51). He quotes John Ziman (1994: 23), whom he describes as "a leading authority on the organization of science," in support of interdisciplinary studies:

> Scientific knowledge now tends to grow particularly vigorously in *interdisciplinary* areas, or to make particularly striking progress when it can be fitted together into a coherent *multidisciplinary*, conceptual scheme.
>
> (Backhouse, 1997: 49)

It would seem that under close scrutiny postmodernism has few critics in the discourse communities of economics and its methodology, philosophy, and history. Yet very few would voluntarily accept the designation of postmodernist. Furthermore, many economists have reported complaints similar to those reported by Robert Solow in his entertaining and penetrating style:

> I don't see how anything but good can come from studying how trained economists actually go about persuading one another. We will learn something about the strategy and tactics of their arguments. Self-knowledge might help to make the arguments better, or at least honest if they are not so ... Nevertheless, I have to report a certain discomfort, a vague itch. It feels like my eclecticism warning me that Klamer and McCloskey are in grave danger of Going Too Far. To be

specific, I worry that their version of the occupational disease is to drift into a belief that one mode of argument is as good as another. In this instance I side with Orwell's pigs: All arguments are equal, but some are more equal than others.

(Solow, 1988: 32–3)

What may be behind Solow's "itch" may have a lot to do with the politics of knowledge in which postmodernism – by virtue of what could be called its holistic approach to the social – is inevitably implicated. Furthermore, the term itself is so vague and over-inclusive that it is probably useless at best. I will attempt to clarify some of the specific taxonomic confusions related to the postmodern in economics in the following section.

Who's afraid of postmodernism?

As part of the welcome re-evaluation of the narratives and meta-narratives structuring the received history of science and economics, there is a need for an increasingly close and critical examination of the secondary texts on which our understanding relies significantly. It simply is not sufficient to rely on a few interdisciplinary applications to form any serious understanding of completely alien modes of inquiry. As McCloskey often declares: One must do one's homework. It is of course true that the rapid disciplinary speciation (the formation of new and distinct species in the course of evolution) following the scientific revolution of the seventeenth century makes it extremely hard for a scholar to master multiple disciplines. Nevertheless, it is precisely this difficulty that must be addressed if the mechanisms that have made modern science what it is are to remain active in modern science. Otherwise, we might find ourselves experiencing diminishing returns to our scholarly efforts in a world characterized by specialization *without trade*.

Before we can discuss the uses and abuses of scientific metaphor in critical theory, we must examine the general workings of metaphors in philosophy. Metaphors are traditionally viewed as contingent elements of philosophical and scientific discourse. They are viewed as useful but essentially distinct from the concepts they are employed to elucidate. Distinguishing between rhetoric and content by recognizing and interpreting metaphors has been a major (if not *the* major) task of philosophy from Aristotle's *Topics* through Wittgenstein and the Vienna Circle. The problem is that "not only is it difficult to find concepts that are not metaphorical, but the very terms in which one defines this philosophical task are themselves metaphorical" (Culler, 1982: 147). In his "White Mythology" Derrida writes:

The values of concept, *foundation*, and *theory* are metaphorical and resist a meta-metaphorical analysis. We need not insist on the optical metaphor that opens under the sun every theoretical point of view. The "fundamental" involves the desire for firm and final ground, for building land, the ground as support for an artificial structure ... Finally, the concept of concept cannot fail to retain, though it would not be reducible to, the pattern of that gesture of power, the taking-now, the grasping and taking hold of the thing as an object.

...

[T]he appeal to criteria of clarity and obscurity [Aristotle's *Topics*] would be enough to establish the point made above: that this whole philosophical delimitation of metaphor is already constructed and worked upon by "metaphors." How could a piece of knowledge or language be clear or obscure *properly* speaking? All the concepts which have played a part in the delimitation of metaphor always have an origin and a force which are themselves "metaphorical."

(Derrida, 1977a: 23–4, 54)

In discussing the difference between content and form, we must remember that deconstruction's double-science is not a revocation of distinctions – between science and its rhetoric for example – but *a more rigorous examination of the functioning of the entire oppositional axis.*

There may be no way for philosophy to free itself from rhetoric, since there seems no way to judge whether or not it has freed itself, the categories for such a judgment being inextricably entwined with the matter to be judged ... The distinction between the literal and the figurative, essential to discussions of the functioning of language, works differently when the deconstructive reversal identifies literal language as figures whose figurality has been forgotten instead of treating figures as deviations from proper, normal literality.

(Culler, 1982: 148, 150)

From a structural point of view, metaphor has a crucial function in scientific inquiry: It is the medium of exchange – the principle characteristic of money – for the mechanism of *consilience*. This term was first coined in 1840 by William Whewell as "Consilience of Inductions" in his *Philosophy of the Inductive Sciences*:

[T]he cases in which induction from classes of facts altogether different have thus *jumped together*, belong only to the best established theories which the history of science contains. And, as I shall have occasion to refer to this particular feature in their evidence, I will take the liberty of describing it by a particular phrase; and will term it the *Consilience of Inductions*.

(Whewell, 1840, in the Oxford English Dictionary under "consilience")

In his *History of the Inductive Sciences*, the man who invented the term "scientist" in 1833 argues that "such coincidences, or consiliences ... are the test of truth" (Whewell, 1847, Vol. 2: 582). Consilience is a pre-positivist structural extension of Aristotelian a priori commonsense truth and has been exceptionally fruitful in natural sciences and especially biology (see Ruse, 1975 and 1998, and Kitcher, 1981). Bringing together disparate areas of inquiry under one unifying principle works, in the words of the historian and philosopher of biology Michael Ruse, in the following way:

> On the one hand, the unifying principle throws explanatory light on the various sub-areas. On the other hand, the sub-areas combine to give credence to the unifying principle. Indeed, argued Whewell, you can thus have confidence in the truth of the principle, even without direct sensory evidence. Much as in a law-court, where one assigns guilt indirectly through circumstantial evidence, so in science you move beyond speculation indirectly through its circumstantial evidence.
>
> (Ruse, 1998: 2)

A thorough contextual evaluation of postmodern ideas with their often-subtle effects on our understanding of science, society, and economics is perhaps still out of our reach – we must go beyond the "post-" to find a new "ism" before gaining sufficient perspective. However, immediate benefit will be gained from much more modest excavations into the historical formations of knowledge. In this text, for example, I have attempted to converse with McCloskey on an explicitly rhetorical level and have been particularly interested in deepening the excavations she had initiated. The reader is probably painfully aware that I have been forced to sacrifice some of the analytical coherence required by a rounded synthetic argument, in favor of engaging the literary dimension of economics on its own literary terms.

Such a rhetorically aware and self-reflexive project must address the political dimension of the postmodern with respect to the confusing diversity among postmodern "practitioners." This is necessary as a counterpoint to the accusations I have made concerning the use of "straw-woman" rhetorical devices in attacks on postmodernism. The politically correct overtones emanating from my coinage of "straw-woman" are quite intentional. It is useful in historical accounts of post-positivism to distinguish between postmodernism and political correctness. Politically correct postmodernists have diverged significantly from the writings of Foucault, Derrida, Deleuze, and other non-P.C. thinkers. That in itself is no sin were it not for the overall shoddiness of the works in question. I confidently pass judgment with my postmodern credentials intact since, as should be clear by now, stratified and contextual internal criticism is not only possible, but indeed *empowered* by a Foucauldian or Derridian postmodernism. I have pointed out several of the major weaknesses of naive – to use a gentler word – postmodernism throughout this text. The principal meta-theoretical mistake they make is in attempting to *replace* the foundations they undermine with new and improved politically correct foundations. This of course completely invalidates the very point of postmodern analysis that, as we have seen, attempts to *study* and foreground the functioning of the foundations in metaphysical systems of knowledge. Derrida writes:

> What has always interested me the most, what has always seemed to me the most rigorous (theoretically, scientifically, philosophically, but also for writing that would no longer be only theoretical-scientific-philosophical), is not indeterminacy in itself, but the strictest possible determination of the figures of play, of oscillation, of undecidability, which is to say, of the *différantial* conditions of determinable history.
>
> ...
>
> [I]t will be understood that the value of truth (and all those values associated with it) is never contested or destroyed in my writing, but only reinscribed in more powerful, larger, more stratified contexts.
>
> (Derrida, 1977b: 145–6)

Though hardly suffering from an excess of false modesty or cautious understatements, this is a far cry from politically correct postmodernism which, as ably explained by Sofianou (1995), founded on an anthropomorphic fallacy similar to positivism (see above). In other words, it is just as metaphysical as positivism without being critically aware of its inevitable auto-deconstructive predicament. "[They] are dispossessed of the longed-for presence in the gesture of language by which [they] attempt to seize it" (Derrida, 1976: 141).

The Sokal hoax

The problem with sloppy pop-science has been put under the spotlight by the notorious "Sokal hoax" in which a prominent physicist – Alan Sokal – published a contrived paper designed to test and expose a leading postmodern journal's uncritical thirst for "hard" scientific justification. It is important to note that Sokal was (and is) very sympathetic to postmodernism in the philosophy of science and intended not to discredit it but to cure it from its tendency for uncritical science-envy. The paper was replete with sexy modern theoretical physics term-dropping including much talk of the uncertainty principle, quantum fluctuations, etc. It appeared in *Social Text* published by Duke University Press and was titled: "Transgressing the Boundaries: Towards a Transformative Hermeneutics of Quantum Gravity" (Sokal, 1996) – no less! Based on all this cutting-edge science, the paper advanced a rather trivial relativistic view of the universe and the humans inhabiting it. The reactions from both sides of "The Science Wars" (*The Economist*, December 13, 1997) were livid: Modernists regarded it as *proof* that postmodern thought is pathetic at best, if not fraudulent, while postmodern thinkers sulked that they too could use language and terms that physicists would find confusing. Naturally, both of these conclusions are misguided if emotionally understandable.

Once the pleasurable snickering is over, the most hard-nosed scientist cannot maintain that publishing a lousy paper immediately invalidates an entire mode of inquiry; science would be thoroughly and repeatedly debunked if that were the case. On the other side of the trenches, English professors must recognize the sobering effect of the hoax and draw some critical conclusions about the uses and abuses of scientific metaphors. Unfortunately this has not yet happened, with the exception of a book titled *Impostures Intellectualles* (Sokal and Bricmont, 1997, US translation: *Fashionable Nonsense: Postmodern Intellectuals' Abuse of Science*, 1998), co-authored by the same relentless Sokal. The book surveys the abuses of scientific metaphors and language in general at the hands of erudite postmodernists. His book is certainly discourse-ethical in that he does not claim to debunk the validity of his protagonists' ideas but only to inform them (and the public) that their *science* is wrong. Interestingly enough Derrida's texts are left entirely out of the book except for a comment in the introduction stating that they are too complicated and do not really have abusive scientific terminology. Whatever one thinks of Derrida's work, sloppiness is the last adjective that can be assigned to it.

A common response on behalf of the postmodern English professors was unfortunately indignation. I was enrolled in a doctoral-level seminar about Derrida at the University of North Carolina at Chapel Hill under the instruction of the eminent English professor Thomas Cohen when the hoax was published and thus found myself behind enemy lines when the bomb hit. I was the only quasi-scientist in the group of doctoral students from the departments of English, philosophy, cultural studies, communication, and different language departments when a colleague from the philosophy department – Nietzschean incidentally – and myself requested that we abandon that evening's three-hour monologue to discuss the hoax, Professor Cohen remarked that he saw no point in this since the hoax was no more than a confidence trick in which a specialist tricks his readers with erroneous material from a discipline they cannot evaluate on a professional level. When we insisted that the paper in fact did not include wrong physics but *third-rate philosophy*, Cohen sneeringly added that he was not surprised and that he did not even intend to read it! Cohen performed what I would call a "Searlism" after the distinguished speech-act theorist and philosopher John R. Searle, who repeatedly shows scant respect for anything but his own particular positions. Searle has become one of deconstruction's major antagonists following his misunderstanding of Derrida's (admiring) critique of John Austin. Since then

Searle has appointed himself chief inquisitor of all things smacking of postmodernism.

Framing the internal with the external

Derrida confronted Searle's criticism in "Limited Inc a b c" (Derrida, 1977b) by carefully showing Searle's arguments to be maliciously ignorant to all but a religiously Searlian reading. But I'm jumping ahead of myself. Speech-act theory was initially articulated by John Austin (though the actual coinage is John Searle's) in his seminal *How to Do Things with Words* (1962). Austin uses the logic of supplementarity to propose a distinction between what he calls constative utterances – the familiar positive statements which, at least in principle, are either true or false – and performative utterances – the supplementary statements that fail to actually state anything but perform an action instead. The meaning of the utterance "can you solve this polynomial?" does not depend on the speaker's consciousness but on conventional rules that relate context and intonation with actions. It is these rules that determine whether the question is rhetorical, confrontational, or a cry of anguish.

Austin finds multiple acts in an utterance: The locutionary act of sounding the utterance, the illocutionary act of inquiring, complaining, warning, stating, etc., and the perlocutionary act, which is the potential action that may be generated by the locutionary and illocutionary acts of the utterance (receiving help with the polynomial, for example). Austin uses the logic of supplementarity (in a Derridian sense) in that he shows that the traditionally perceived primary function of statements: To state facts (constative utterances), is in fact a special case of the supplemental or marginal class of performative utterances. Consider the statement: "the present value of lifetime income is the most important determinant of current consumption." A constative utterance if ever there was one. Now add the words "I wish to persuade you that ..." at the beginning of the statement and you have a "performative of persuasion." Add to this "I hereby state that ..." at the beginning and it's a "performative of fact-stating" that is identical to the original constative utterance in its own terms, yet is a subcategory of a large class of performative utterances. Austin studies illocutionary acts by looking at the conventions that make it possible for performative utterances to fail.

Derrida finds Austin's work – like Saussure's – to be splendidly autodeconstructive. He discusses this reading of speech-act theory in *Signature Event Context* (1977a). Derrida shows that in *How to Do Things with Words* (1962) Austin reintroduces metaphysical presence into his system when he insists that the utterances under investigation must be spoken and taken "seriously" (intriguingly, the quotation marks are Austin's). This exclusion emerges as early as page nine and is addressed in several instances with varying degrees of apologetic discomfort. Non-serious

utterances such as those produced by an actor on stage are peculiar for
Austin.

> Language in such circumstances is in special ways – intelligibly – used
> not seriously, but in ways parasitic upon its normal use – ways which
> fall under the doctrine of the etiolations of language. All this we are
> excluding from consideration.
>
> (Austin, 1962: 21–2)

Derrida's essay engendered a strong reaction from the reigning authority
on speech-act theory. In "Reiterating the Differences: A Reply to
Derrida" (1977), Searle reaffirms an *ersatz* version of Austin's auto-
deconstructive move. I am relieved to note that such an unsophisticated
version of positive analytical philosophy is rarely encountered in our
profession today:

> Austin correctly saw that it was necessary to hold in abeyance one set
> of questions, about parasitic discourse, until one has answered a logi-
> cally prior set of questions about "serious" discourse ... The existence
> of the pretended form of the speech act is logically dependent on the
> possibility of the nonpretended speech act in the same way that any
> pretended form of behavior is dependent on nonpretended forms of
> behavior, and in this sense the pretended forms are parasitical on the
> nonpretended forms.
>
> (Searle, 1977: 204–5)

Happily, most economists – allow me to be optimistic – would not ridicule
themselves by stating, for example, that behavior that is not fully rational in
the economic sense is to be excluded from investigation because it is parasit-
ical on the rational consumer choice model. Alternatively, perhaps we should
ignore market imperfections because they are logically dependent on perfectly competitive general equilibrium models. Ignoring anomalies can never
be a reasonable policy for science or inquiry of any kind in the long run.

Derrida reads Austin very seriously (no quotation marks here) and
observes that his anxious exclusion of "parasitic discourse" is not necessarily a problem once it is deconstructed: Its paradoxical hierarchy is at least
temporarily neutralized. A speech-act such as a promise is made possible
by iterable procedures that apply both on and off the stage. These procedures are related to the very role-playing that Austin and Searle are so
anxious to exclude:

> [F]or the "standard case" of promising to occur, it must be recogniz-
> able as the repetition of a conventional procedure, and the actor's
> performance on the stage is an excellent model of such repetition. The
> possibility of "serious" performatives depends upon the possibility of

performances, because performatives depend upon the iterability that is most explicitly manifested in performances ... Imitation is not an accident that befalls an original but its condition of possibility.

(Culler, 1982: 119–20)

What is it that compels Austin to reintroduce this dubious hierarchical opposition (serious/non-serious) and with it the presence of a signifying intention in the speaker's consciousness? It must be a compelling reason since rejecting such a move – along the constative/performative opposition – was the cornerstone of speech-act theory. The problem is the possibility of grafting utterances onto a context that alters their function, and the possibility of framing contexts. The reader will recall Foucault's critique of René Magritte's painting titled *The Treachery of Images* (1929), which features a pipe suspended in mid air above the written statement *Ceci n'est pas une pipe* (This is not a pipe) (see *The Production of Knowledge*, page 75, and Foucault, 1973/1983). The surrealistic point Magritte is making is precisely about the complex interdependency of context and frame. In our context here, the constative statement taken within the frame of the picture would seem to be false – it is a painting of a pipe and not a "real" pipe. In other words, if we allow the outside of the frame to contaminate the inside, then the statement is true. Context is inherently boundless in that it can always be reinterpreted and broadened. Furthermore, as so elegantly demonstrated by Magritte, a context under investigation can always be grafted onto the context of the investigation and thus engender a new context that escapes that investigation – an infinite regression again. Incidentally, in French the term for an infinite regression is *mise en abyme*, which evokes a space with reflective surfaces which reflect each other infinitely. A common example is a mirrored elevator; think about this next time you find yourself in one.

Derrida also discusses the issue of framing in its relation to judgment in his analysis of Immanuel Kant's *The Critique of Judgment* (1790).

Every analytic or aesthetic judgment presupposes that we can rigorously distinguish between the intrinsic and the extrinsic. Aesthetic judgment *must* concern intrinsic beauty, and not the around and about. It is therefore necessary to know – and this is the fundamental presupposition, the presupposition of the fundamental – how to define the intrinsic, the framed, and what to exclude as frame *and* as beyond the frame ... And since when we ask, "what is a frame?" Kant responds, it is a *parergon*, a composite of inside and outside, but a composite which is not an amalgam or half-and-half but an outside which is called inside the inside to constitute it as inside.

(Derrida, 1978/1979: 53/12)

There is an ontological complication here, which is perhaps the root of Searle's misreading of Derrida. It manifests itself as a paradox: The *parergon* paradox arises when we notice that the framing device that signals genre is itself not a member of that genre. For example, the archive of knowledge is not knowledge and knowledge is not the archive. More particularly, writing that McCloskey lacks a serious engagement with the epistemological underpinnings of her work is not a serious engagement with the epistemological underpinnings of her work, and vice versa. This is related to Tarascio's (1975, 1997) discussions on levels of inquiry that I have mentioned before, but, as we have become accustomed to expect, the gaps are displaced. While Tarascio takes the traditional approach consisting of distinguishing *between* levels of inquiry, Derrida looks at distinctions operating *within* each level. The two are compatible, and have the added advantage of being able to examine differences between differences: how inter-level and intra-level distinctions relate to each other and to the concepts they distinguish between.

The distinction between criticism and the text it criticizes is a distinction between a discourse of the outside, meta-language, and a discourse of the inside: language. Culler recognizes that the authority of a critic's meta-linguistic position depends significantly on the meta-linguistic discourse within the work:

> They [critics] feel securely outside and in control when they can bring out of the work passages of apparently authoritative commentary that expound the views they are defending. When reading a work that apparently lacks an authoritative metalanguage or that ironically questions the interpretive discourses it contains, critics feel uneasy, as if they were just adding their voice to the polyphony of voices. They lack evidence that they are indeed in a metalinguistic position, above and outside of the text ... In denying their externality we subvert the metalinguistic authority of the critic, whose externality had depended on the folds that created this internal metalanguage or pocket of externality. The distinction between language and metalanguage, like the distinction between inside and outside, evades precise formulation but is always at work, complicating itself in a variety of folds.
>
> (Culler, 1982: 199)

The Mäki–McCloskey debate is an excellent example of the disconcerting effects the lack of meta-linguistic or external positions have on criticism. McCloskey's analytically shaky epistemology is displaced by Mäki who brings them under the harsh light of analytical philosophy. When McCloskey attempts to counter the perceived threat by questioning the very legitimacy of the *displacement*, she is in fact reaffirming the shakiness of her epistemology. In general, I am referring to how problematic aspects in a text are often reflected in the secondary literature (a conceptual frame of sorts) when complex multiplicities are forcibly refined down to a monism or singularity which drives a specific reading. Looking at the secondary literature is crucial for deconstruction.

My problem with Searle is with the lack of respect for intellectual traditions and the celebration of ignorance. McCloskey recounts how she once personally asked Searle how he would fit Hegel into his brave new scheme:

> "I have never read a page of Hegel; and furthermore, I propose never to do so." The reply evoked gales of laughter from the philosophy graduate students gathered around the great man, who thus exhibited his disdain from the considered judgment of half his culture.
>
> (McCloskey, 1992: 266)

The prohibition of non-scientific language has led, as any economist would expect, to the creation of an underground rhetorical economy. All the suppressed linguistic complications re-enter the system as implicit rhetorical devices and strategies that, more often than not, are not even directly motivated by the author (insofar as such motivation is at all possible). The price that has been paid for a supposedly pure scientific discourse is thus a complete loss of control over the suppressed discursive forces at play.

But not all is rotten in the postmodern kingdom, and the Political Correctness *shibboleth* has come under increasing attacks from within its own discursive community. I would argue that a significant degree of confusion is still rampant in postmodern circles today, but that this paradigmatic incommensurability can be, and is already being, reduced by careful rational study. What is unfortunate is that denunciative politically correct postmodern offshoots are, almost by definition, more flamboyant and cavalier, and tend to attract devastating criticisms that are then attached to significant work by association. One of the most flamboyant examples given by Sokal and Bricmont comes from the literary sub-genre of feminist criticism. Luce Irigaray (1987: 110, in Sokal and Bricmont 1997: 104) supports her claim that science is "sexualized" by interpreting Einstein's iconoclastic equation relating matter and energy ($E = MC^2$) as "privileging" the speed of light over "other speeds" because light, in its speediness, is a male value. I wholeheartedly agree with Irigaray that science is sexualized *via its institutions*, but I am not sure that she is looking for it in the right places. More importantly, I'm unconvinced that such analysis advances the feminist agenda in the sciences. At any rate, I hope to have convinced the reader that postmodernism, at the very least, cannot be reduced to crude textualism, and that it can inform science.

Texts and (hi)stories

Derrida is often accused of being a *textualist* by those who find themselves often accused of being *historicists*. The distinction revolves around whether one accepts that historical context determines meaning. Derrida's problem – it should be clear by now – is with the determination of meaning, not the march of history. History should not be an exogenous foundation or presence, but must be endogenized; made part of the workings of the model. Time is in fact an important tool for deconstruction since it serves to undermine foundations in general via the deferral in *différance*:

> We shall distinguish by the term différance, the movement by which language, or any code, any system of reference in general, becomes "historically" constituted as a fabric of differences ... If the word history did not carry with it the theme of a final repression of difference, we could say that differences alone could be "historical" through and through and from the start.
>
> (Derrida, 1972a/1977: 12)

The first step in recognizing metaphysical presence is to see it "à partir du temps comme différance"; in relation to time as difference, differing, and deferral (Derrida, 1976: 166). In Culler's words:

> Derrida uses history against philosophy: when confronted with essentialist, idealizing theories and claims to ahistorical or transhistorical understanding, he asserts the historicity of these discourses and theoretical assumptions. But he also uses philosophy against history and the claims of historical narratives ... [Which are used] to control the meaning of rich and complex works by ruling out possible meanings as historically inappropriate.
>
> (Culler, 1982: 129)

This historically constituted "fabric of differences" is the generalized text (*archi-écriture*), a text that includes time in its structure. Phenomenologists and sophisticated realists may object that Wittgenstein had already noted the arbitrary nature of what he called the language game and that interpretation and determination of meaning is a real fact of human existence. This brings us back to the question of interpretation if we are to gain some understanding of the production of meaning.

Derrida lists two interpretations of interpretation that "divide the field which we call, so problematically, the human sciences":

> The one seeks to decipher, dreams of deciphering a truth or an origin which escapes play and the order of the sign and which lives the necessity of interpretation as an exile. The other, which is no longer turned toward the origin, affirms play and tries to pass beyond man and humanism, the name of man being the name of the being who, throughout the history of metaphysics and of onto-theology – in other

words, throughout his entire history – has dreamed of full presence, of reassuring foundation, of the origin and the end of play ... I do not for my part believe, although these two interpretations must accentuate their difference and sharpen their irreducibility, that there can today be any question of choosing – in the first place because here we are in a region (let us say, provisionally, of historicity) where the notion of choice is particularly trivial; and in the second place because we must first try to conceive of the common ground and the Différance of this irreducible difference.

(Derrida, 1967/1978: 427–8/292–3)

Choice here is trivial because "the language of theory always leaves a residue that is neither formalizable nor idealizable in terms of that theory of language" (Derrida 1988: 209). If we are to accept that determined meaning is always subject to the language game of interpretation and re-contextualization, yet eschew the philosophical Dadaism relativists are often accused of, we must consider the meaning of meaning. Derrida is wondering whether

the meaning of meaning (in the most general sense of meaning and not of indication) is infinite implication? The unchecked referral from signifier to signifier? If its force is a certain pure and infinite equivocal-ness, which gives signified meaning no respite, no rest, but engages it within its own economy to go on signifying and to differ/defer?

(Derrida, 1967/1978: 42/25)

Even though – regardless of our language-theory choice – we are always confronted with a non-determinable *residue*, this is no reason to abandon a theory or theory in general. Residues have been a part of science from its magical beginnings to its current state through which most of us view the world today: from the Christian inquiry into free will, through Gödel's demonstration of the incompleteness of mathematics, to the current inquiry into the quantum structure of the universe and its inception.

5 Refutation

Beyond ethical neutrality

Why use deconstruction?

It is often said that deconstruction is no longer even fashionable among critical and literary theorists and should thus be left to historians of literary theory. I would strongly caution against such a view for two reasons. First, as we have seen above, deconstruction is an interpretative process that has been used for millennia (e.g. Zeno and the Plato–Sophist debate) whether consciously or not. In the chapter "The genealogy of postmodernism" (Cullenberg et al., 2001: 102–28), McCloskey tells the cyclical story of the longest argument in western civilization between realists and relativists, and argues that postmodernism is the current flavor of the relativist position. My second reason for cautioning against the abandonment of deconstruction is that deconstruction can be confidently regarded as the most important paradigm in postmodern thought: an irreducible view of structure to which most other theories can be readily reduced. There are intriguing new variants of deconstruction and novel approaches in different disciplines, but they all eventually auto-deconstruct like everything else (consciously or not).

One of the more intriguing things McCloskey states is that as economists we are particularly well placed to assimilate critical theory into our view of the world. She argues that the complexity of economic phenomena has made economists particularly aware of the shortcomings of positive dogma in the business of *doing* economics. This is in fact the basis of her distinction between economists and economic methodologists, the latter being the alleged torchbearers of modernism in economics. This has been picked up by Jane Rossetti in her pioneering "Deconstructing Robert Lucas" (1990) where she proceeds to perform a textbook deconstruction of the hugely influential "Lucas Critique" articulated by the Nobel laureate Robert Lucas (Lucas, 1976). Rossetti's paper received hardly any serious responses beyond sporadic references ostensibly remarking that economic texts *can* be deconstructed which, as should be clear by now, is a triviality. Even McCloskey in her commentary on Rossetti (1990) and Mirowski (1990) remarks that Rossetti has "done her homework" unlike

Mirowski but is running the risk of scarring economists with the D-word. Rossetti attempted to update her paper (Rossetti, 1992) by elaborating a little more about how her deconstruction is – like any deconstruction – already inscribed in the object-text itself and functions as a structural critique, but again no fruitful reactions ensued. Sadly, Rossetti has given up on academic economics and the discipline has lost an original thinker.

Rossetti's choice of the Lucas Critique is very astute. The auto-deconstructive structure of the Critique is familiar to economists since it is *the very point Lucas is trying to make*. The Critique argues that economists are wrong to base policy recommendations on a static structural model representing the economy since the policies they propose would themselves inevitably change the structure of the economy due to public expectations, thus rendering the policies no longer appropriate. The result of intervention would be increased noise in the system with no way of determining the outcomes, and thus no way of designing good economic policies. When he talks of structural parameters shifting due to expectations and thus invalidating predictions based on the original parameters, he is talking about a structure of difference and deferral (*différance*). As in the paradox of structures (languages, theoretical models) and events (words, empirical observations), here too we have a conceptual structure that captures both the passive pre-existing economic structures as well as the active event of anticipation that produces them (see *Proof* above). In the case of the Lucas Critique, the paradox can be stated as follows: General macroeconomic models are composed of a group of economic variables such as investment and interest rates, and specified relationships between these variables. These relationships (or coefficients) are however constantly changing because they deal with highly complex social relations in the economy. An observation at a *specific* time and place can be incorporated into the *general* model meaningfully only by relying on prior observations on which the model is based. The model is, after all, made of such prior observations and the relationships that existed between them in the past. When one attempts to use such a model to determine how specific policies affecting one variable (interest rates for example) could manipulate another (investment for example), one runs into a paradox similar to the language-general/word-specific paradox discussed in the *Proof* above: Changing a variable will affect its relationships with other variables because people and institutions will react to this intervention by modifying their behavior and thus the general model will no longer represent the economy accurately (if it ever did initially). The attempts of the policy makers to control specific outcomes are just as futile as the analytical philosopher trying to control the exact meaning of a complex discursive construct (such as truth). Once the policy is enacted, the world in which that policy was designed to operate becomes a different world and thus, to paraphrase Voltaire's Professor Pangloss, even the best of all policies will fail when it is no longer in the best of all possible worlds.

Lucas has thus grafted the theory of rational expectations onto neo-classical economics in a structural *intervention* that was instrumental in its rise to pre-eminence. The Critique questioned the very possibility of deter-mining a policy's consequence, much like deconstruction's denial of the possibility of determining a text's meaning. Both signal an era in that no further work could proceed as if it had never happened. In fact, it would seem that most economists converted *en block* to rational-expectations-augmented-neoclassicism and the study of macroeconomic policy became a study of why policy never works. Economists, of course, are intimately familiar with the Lucas Critique and vaguely familiar with postmodernism. Non-economists know, in most likelihood, nothing of the Critique, and are perhaps just as confused by postmodern philosophy. I strongly suspect that the brush-fire spread of the Lucas Critique in economics is precisely because it is a deconstruction. Of course, there are also the aesthetic, ana-lytical, and above all political criteria that certainly favored such an elo-quent articulation of a libertarian position in the late 1970s.

Deconstruction has an impact on a series of critical concepts (text, truth, literature, etc.). Such fundamental concepts are shown to rely on hierarchical oppositions. Applying the logic of deconstruction allows us to view the excluded, supplementary, all but irrelevant, special case as a general case of the "high" concept. Science is thus a particular kind of rhetoric and not a distinct non-rhetorical methodology. Looking at philo-sophical (non-literary, scientific, positive) discourse as a "species" of writing allows Derrida

> to study the philosophic text in its formal structure, its rhetorical organization, the specificity and diversity of its textual types, its models of exposition and production – beyond what were once called genres – and, further, the space of its staging [*mises en scènes*] and its syntax, which is not just the articulation of its signifieds and its refer-ences to being or to truth but also the disposition of its procedures and of everything invested in them. In short, thus to consider philosophy as "a particular literary genre," which draws upon the reserves of lin-guistic system, organizing, forcing, or diverting a set of tropological possibilities that are older than philosophy.
>
> (Derrida, 1972a/1977: 348–9)

Let us then consider economics as a particular literary genre, and apply the procedures of deconstruction to it. The first step could be to look at the epistemological history of the opposition between *general* systematic knowledge (science) and *specific* observations. The reader is by now famil-iar with the workings of such general/specific oppositions such as struc-ture/event and language/word. The general/specific opposition governs the very distinction between theoretical science with its deductive methods and empirical science with its inductive methods.

A critical history of the basic epistemological unit: the fact

The central tension structuring the history of what the cultural critic Mary Poovey (1998) calls "the Modern Fact" since the seventeenth century is between a particular observable event and the abstract structure of systematic knowledge to which it is subjected. Since the fact serves as the basic indivisible epistemological unit, the tension inhabits all discourses of truth including economics. Aristotle was not troubled by conflating events into structures since he defined the capacity to produce knowledge as the ability to do precisely that kind of transformation: observing and recognizing universal commonplaces as foundations for deductive reasoning. Consequently, for most of western thought until the Renaissance, facts depended on a priori self-evident universal commonplaces. When the commonplaces/observations hierarchy was reversed during the Scientific Revolution of the seventeenth century, empirical science emerged as the primary form of explaining our world. It was however not long before David Hume spoiled the fun with his skepticism as to whether it was possible to find deductive theoretical foundations or justifications for using induction at all! We use induction daily, and as a basis for deduced general laws (ethical, scientific, religious, or practical), even though induction itself cannot be placed on an absolute deductive foundation. This continues to plague the modern fact and the knowledge systems that use it as their basic epistemological unit. Deductive logic, inductive techniques, and specific disciplinary rhetoric have repeatedly been employed to justify this leap of faith over Humean skepticism.

In her *A History of the Modern Fact: Problems of Knowledge in the Sciences of Wealth and Society* (1998), Poovey reconstructs the Scientific Revolution as insisting on a role for particular events – as opposed to Aristotelian deduction from commonplaces – in the production of knowledge. Francis Bacon's facts were no longer predicated on the Aristotelian justification of being universal and common. Instead, Baconian facts perform the structural function of justifying theoretical constructs. The concept of the modern fact is itself more than a brute fact: The presence of a factual realm is the link between the inside (consciousness – the realm of theory) and the outside (reality – the realm of fact), and is a fundamental aspect of modern science.

Here is where McCloskey has again pointed us in the right direction. She has increasingly shifted her philosophical interest towards ethics, seemingly neglecting rhetoric altogether. This could be seen as an indication that she has failed in her philosophical engagement with the rhetoric of economics and has prudently selected to focus her intellectual energy on her methodological criticisms of economics and most ardently on the misuse of statistical significance. A closer examination reveals however that McCloskey's ethical move is philosophically necessary in order to engage the problems raised by her philosophical project. Her methodological prescription is a commitment to *sprachethik*. It is however based on an exogenous discourse regime in the form of the academic community whose membership requirements are obviously social and contextual (peer-review is by definition social and even political). It is thus impossible to justify a methodological laissez faire prescription on anything but an ethical commitment to Austrian metaphysics. This is what I believe to be the most severe criticism raised against McCloskey (externally by Mäki and internally in this text). It is also the reason she was forced to assume an idealistic position and define her relative and socially dependent lowercase-t truth as the discourse of an ethical and enlightened elite (to which she herself belongs).

Ethics may yet save the day however, because it is the study of human choice: an absolute decision in relative ignorance. This is precisely what participants in the economic conversation are supposed to adjudicate. Ethics is structured by the tensions between the inside – the subjective self with its interpretations and interests – and the outside, the other, to which we cannot have direct access, and therefore *must* be conceived in ideal form as a Law (scientific, ethical, religious, civic, or otherwise).

Economics and ethics

In their survey of ethical values in economics, Charles Wilber and Roland Hoksbergen (1986) recognize three locations in which ethics has entered into economic discourse: Economic agents subscribe to ethical imperatives in the business of doing business, economic institutions and policies do not have uniform effects on people and thus ethical evaluations are involved in their evolution and evaluation, and economists subscribe to ethical imperatives in the business of doing economics. The role of ethics in individual agents' decision-making has received some attention in the 1990s. Jerry Evensky (1993), for example, studies the ethical underpinnings of Adam Smith's concept of the invisible hand. Specifically, Evensky looks at the sensitivity of the achievement of the common good to the assumption that most agents are not only motivated by self-interest but are also constrained by internalized moral laws. Consequently, he draws two major conclusions: First, economic agents are dually motivated by their specific interests as well as by the ethical imperatives enforced by their society. Second, economic efficiency requires internalized ethical behavior, which excludes well-defined economic phenomena such as the free-rider problem, and moral hazard.

Those economists who are committed to utility theory yet choose not to disregard these complications have been attempting to formally incorporate moral values into their work. The first approach is to treat internalized morality as altruistic preferences and incorporate these into the utility function. In his *Trattato* (1916), Pareto worked with matrices of simultaneous utility functions in which each agent's utility was derived from the weighted utilities of all other agents in the economy. Applying intersubjective utility functions (even theoretically) involves an intractable degree of complexity and consequently the approach is almost only discussed at the meta-theoretical level (see Fullbrook, 2002 and George, 2001). Even though it could potentially offer a more satisfying account of preferences than most available models, it only addresses economic behavior that is not self-interested: altruism.

Evaluating economic policy and, more broadly, the institutions with which it interacts, is another ethical dimension of economics that has received some attention. The issue turns around the complex and thickly political concept of *interpersonal comparisons* – already a central problematic in the Aristotelian distinction between distributive (regressive) and commutative (progressive) justice. Neoclassical theoretical economics is enamored with the efficiency criterion named after Vilfredo Pareto, since it provides a convenient formal criterion for evaluating economic outcomes. By defining *Pareto optimality* as the state in which nobody can be made better off without reducing somebody else's wellbeing, interpersonal comparisons are entirely avoided. Tarascio (1968, 1969) has argued that Pareto himself had developed this criterion in order to demonstrate how the influential general-equilibrium theory he helped create would have little value for policy considerations until a sociological theory of intersubjective utility could be developed. It is a sad irony that the rest of the profession misunderstood this methodological caricature and adopted such a Panglossian norm uncritically.

The only sort of policy that can be meaningfully evaluated with Pareto optimality is the kind in which there are no interpersonal tradeoffs. This excludes almost all relevant policy issues since, in the absence of interpersonal tradeoffs, even politicians would be able to enact good policy all by themselves. Painfully aware of this, welfare economists have developed the concept of *potential* Pareto improvement, which only requires that the overall change in utility due to a policy is positive. In the best of all possible worlds, Pareto improvements materialize – as opposed to remaining potential – when "winners" are *required* to share the gains with "losers" by offering compensating payments. One pertinent consequence of this general approach is that, by definition, the domain of ethical considerations is restricted to an evaluation of the economic consequences of a policy *ex post facto* (after the fact and independent of it). Ethics is thus excluded from the scope of economics and relegated to a supplemental political role that is typically assigned to non-economists. The economist-philosophers Daniel Hausman and Michael McPherson argue the following:

> The facts that economists need to know some morality to know what questions to ask, that economists can rarely describe moral commitments without evaluating them, and that economists effect what they see by how they describe it, provide even purely positive economists

with reasons to think about both the morality accepted in the society they study and the morality they think should be accepted. Moral reflection has a role in both normative economics and in much of what is called positive economics. In principle, positive economics might be separable from all evaluative propositions, but positive economists will be influenced by their moral values and their attitudes toward the values of the agents they study.

(Hausman and McPherson, 1994: 256)

The denial of an ethical dimension to economics is part of what defines modernism in physics – "I didn't drop the bomb, I just developed it" – and in economics – "I'm not responsible for economic inequality, I just developed the theory to justify it." The positive/normative opposition supports the ethical mechanism by which scientists disown the ethical consequences of their work.

At the proverbial blackboard, economists are able to design policies that can be evaluated with well-defined criteria. Typically, these are versions of Pareto optimality that are shown to potentially exist given a set of assumptions. Raising the minimum wage, for example, will increase unemployment as well as the welfare of workers. Once analysis leaves the positive world of the blackboard, it becomes apparent that the policy problem itself (to raise or not to raise the minimum wage) cannot be resolved with the theoretical model used to address it. What is missing according to McCloskey (1994) is a "quantitative rhetoric of approximation" to allow economists to evaluate not whether the tradeoff exists, but what are its quantitative effects. In this case, these effects would be the relative size of the rise in unemployment and the increase in workers' welfare. Such rhetoric cannot eschew explicit interpersonal comparisons that neoclassical rhetoric suppresses by displacing them into what Hausman and McPherson (1993, 1994) call a "normative theory of rationality."

The ethical foundations of the theory of rationality

Rationality is minimally defined in economics as having complete (well-defined over the set of all relevant options) and transitive (with coherent and stable rankings) preferences, and that a rational agent's choices are determined by these preferences. The first problem that arises is how to deal with the risk and uncertainty associated with most economic activities. The standard solution is to assume that people can attach correct probabilities to all possible outcomes (agents' subjective beliefs fully conform to a probabilistic framework), and that preferences are not altered by experience (mutually independent from each other). We thus have what is known as *expected* utility theory, but rationality is still defined as having a well-defined, coherent, and stable set of preferences, and rationally maximizing one's welfare or utility simply means making choices according to these preferences. As Hausman and McPherson put it:

> [T]he identification of the actual with the rational remains. It does not depend on any particular formulation. It is, rather, a reflection of the fact that economics simultaneously provides a theory of causes and consequences of people's economic choices and of the reasons for them ... [T]he positive theory of choice is simultaneously a theory of rational choice and thereby serves to evaluate even as it predicts and explains agents' conduct.
>
> (Hausman and McPherson, 1994: 258–9)

This tautology strongly supports positive theory against the most devastating falsifying instances. The assumption that people's preferences are transitive and complete has been repeatedly and powerfully falsified both from a theoretical perspective (cognitive psychology) and from an experimental perspective (see for example Vernon Smith, Charles Holt, and others' work in experimental game theory). This however is conveniently resolved by using the normative theory of choice to declare all such behavioral phenomena as irrational and unstable and thus not within the domain of positive science. On the surface, it would seem that this is no longer the case with experimental game-theorists being traded like professional athletes (I've been told that graduate student assistantships have been capped until George Mason University can finish financing the recent arrival of Vernon Smith from the University of Arizona).

Digging below the surface of economic theory reveals that a normative theory of choice (along with other rhetorical devices) is part of the system that supports McCloskey's prescription for *herrschaftsfrei sprachethik* (dominance-free discourse ethic) with its underlying Austrian metaphysics. The irrational, unstable, and otherwise marginal behavior is recognized but safely quarantined within the category of *supplemental* phenomena, allowing the hard-core disciplinary principles that would be destabilized by them to proceed with business as usual.

To understand this system and thus McCloskey's theoretical and metatheoretical position I use Hausman and McPherson's (1994) study of the ethical stakes that economics holds in a specific normative theory of choice (see *Appendix II: The ethical strata in economic theory*, page 127). They proceed by deriving normative economics from the theory of rationality augmented by the typical assumptions that agents are exclusively self-interested and have perfect knowledge. The first auxiliary assumption establishes that agents prefer what they believe to be better for them. The second assumption assures that an agent's beliefs are true and thus leads to the familiar normative principle according to which *welfare is the same as satisfying preferences*. From an economist's perspective, the essentially problematic issue of making interpersonal welfare comparisons is thus wholly avoided because what are being compared are different degrees of preference-satisfaction that are structurally identified with welfare. A rhetorician of economics may however wonder what societal consequences might develop from the pervasive acceptance of the onanistic idea that happiness is nothing more than self-gratification.

From a model-builder's perspective however, so far so good. All that is needed now is the uncontroversial assumption of "minimal benevolence" according to which other people's economic welfare is morally good – *ceteris paribus* (all else held constant) of course. Consequently, normative economics should evaluate whether economic institutions and policies allow individuals to satisfy their preferences. As we have seen however the vital and controversial assumption in this deductive chain is not minimal benevolence but the seemingly straightforward assumption that maximizing one's economic welfare is identical to satisfying one's preferences. The Nobel laureate economist-philosopher Amartya Sen (1973) has argued against the latter assumption based on conceptually broad counter-examples: People make mistakes (even with excellent information; let alone without it), people have preferences regarding tradeoffs between personal wellbeing and other goals, and people have wants that are motivated by various reasons, only one of which is economic wellbeing. Analytically circumventing these problems requires both the assumptions of perfect information (everybody knows everything) and exclusive self-interest (pure egoism). To justify these radical assumptions both rhetorically and ethically – implicitly of course since such discourses are not "legitimate" science – the profession has adopted the word "rational" to signify the crucial assumptions of exclusive self-interest with perfect information. Hausman and McPherson note in passing that in ordinary speech rational is often synonymous with prudence. The concept of prudence has an important history in classical economics and nineteenth century thought in general. McCloskey (1996) has noted the central role this concept played in ancient and Victorian ethics and consequently in classical economic ethics. The cultural perspective supports the analytical conclusions of Hausman and McPherson: Establishing a moral imperative that only prudent behavior is rational is a major moral commitment that supports the entire deductive chain on which virtually all choice theories in economics depend. Not surprisingly, the historical and cultural context in which modern economics evolved have left traces stratified like fossils in the analytical deductive structure of the discipline. Ignoring these traces while adopting the deductive structure leads to what amounts to ethical adhockery.

Deductively deriving normative economics from the theory of rationality does not suggest better foundations for the theory of choice, but it does allow us to locate, illuminate, and explain the ethical underpinnings of both positive and normative economics, and the specific moral commitments of our discipline. An important application would be to the functioning of the concept of *competition* that plays a significant role in both academic and political discourse. The prevalent ethical commitment to competition in general is based on establishing perfect competition as an ethical good because, with the first and second welfare theorems, it guarantees preference satisfaction and thus maximizes welfare. The first welfare theorem states that perfectly competitive equilibria are Pareto optimal (efficient) and thus, given minimal benevolence, a moral good. At this point, the deductive chain becomes a strong defense of the very narrow stylized technical concept of *perfect* competition. That perfect competition is Pareto efficient is acceptable to most economists throughout the political and professional spectrum. Whether it has ever actually existed is another matter. The second welfare theorem is the last step towards establishing perfect competition as an ethical imperative at the center of orthodox economics. It states that all Pareto optima can be obtained as competitive equilibria from some initial distribution of endowments (principally skills and resources). Much like the related concept of potential Pareto improvements, initial endowments are extremely hard to manipulate in actuality, and it is even doubtful that they are conceptually tractable given the problematic nature of what is exactly meant by initial in the context of an evolving economy.

This in itself does not present a problem if it is accompanied with a healthy dose of skepticism concerning the applicability of policies directly derived from the general-equilibrium model. Unfortunately, the recent history of economics' explicit ethical commitment to competition hides a deformed sibling in the attic: the implicit moral position that views competition as a good in itself regardless of consequences (deontologically, as opposed to consequentially). Ignoring or misunderstanding the complex ethical structure of our discipline gives rise to damaging interpretations in popular political culture, and has misled some economists into making errors in policy proposals with devastating effects on multitudes of people. One needs but mention the prescription of "shock therapy" to post-communist economies in transition (the Chubais privatization plan in Russia in the 1990s is an excellent case in point), the prescriptions of the International Monetary Fund for developing countries seeking funds, as well as many examples of supposedly competition-promoting legislation leading to increased monopoly power.

The practice of directly drawing actual policy recommendations from purely theoretical models without recognizing that such a transfer is – at the very least – problematic is not that new. Joseph Schumpeter called it the "Ricardian Vice" and McCloskey calls it "the futility of blackboard economics." Where I believe this problem most urgently bites is in its rhetorical dimension. Academic prescriptions that are developed and understood in an academic context are then translated into the lay language of politics, losing much of their nuance by the time that they are applied. I already mentioned that little is left of the sophistication of the "discretion versus rules" debate in macroeconomic theory when Milton Friedman's "3 percent monetary growth rule" is interpreted by policy makers and talking heads. The arguments are further debased when we ignore their historical context and role within the age-old American debate between Hamilton and Jefferson over centralized economic policy. As economists, we are understandably loath to assume responsibility for the actual outcomes of our learned opinions as they enter onto the political arena. The no man's land in which our work is translated into actual economic policy needs significant further study. I highly recommend James Arnt Aune's *Selling the Free Market: The Rhetoric of Economic Correctness* (2001) which is a forerunner in this vein. My one reservation is that Aune does not do justice to McCloskey even though he dedicates an appendix to her. He reiterates the criticism (discussed by Mäki, others, and myself) of her ethical advocacy of competition in the marketplace of ideas, what I call her Austrian metaphysics. The deductive foundations of this metaphysical system have been laid down by Hausman and McPherson and my extensions thereof (see *Appendix II*). It is useful to follow McCloskey's ethical focus and take a tentative deconstructive look at ethics, its structure, and its functions. For this purpose, I will start by locating, reversing, and employing the now familiar general/specific opposition in the context of ethical thought.

Specific moral acts and the general structure of ethics

Ethics promises to answer questions arising from an inevitable human dilemma: One has to make specific decisions based on universal laws or principles in an uncertain world. The literary theorist Geoffrey Galt Harpham (1992, 1995) suggests that there is a fundamental incommensurability between the two questions that dominate ethical inquiry: "how ought one live?" and "what ought I to do?" Answered separately, they are themselves unethical or even impossible since the first requires a detached godlike perspective, while the second implies complete self-absorption. Both questions are necessary for an ethical decision but the decision itself is made without fully answering the two questions. In the jargon of formal logic: An ethical decision is *over*-determined by the structurally different specific and general questions. At the same time, ethical reasoning is predicated on norms that are to be accepted or rejected as such – ethical reasoning is logically *under*-determined by the answers. That is why ethical questions involve emotional and ideological elements and cannot be fully resolved by logical reasoning. The age-old debate between the realists and the relativists is the persistent thorn in modern philosophy's side precisely because any system of knowledge is both over-determined and under-determined by reality. The former is due to the existence of unexplained and debated observed phenomena, and the latter is a result of the necessary set of presuppositions, ideological commitments, and beliefs that are part of even the hardest of sciences. This cannot be resolved but must nevertheless be *endured* in the Nietzschean sense of a transformative undergoing (*untergehen*).

The apparent logical under-determination of ethical choice conceals its structural *over*-determination and implies another choice: a choice between different principles. Viewing the ethical dimension as structured by the *general* imperative to make ethical choices, and the *specific* moral principles on which one acts, has an important implication. Ethics has the same structural duplicity as the hierarchical oppositions that it governs: Ethics requires taking a moral position in order to come to a decision and be ethical, but moral positions necessarily refer to ethical authority to be moral.

Darwinian ethics

Adam Smith's concept of the invisible hand assumes that most agents are motivated not only by self-interest but according to internalized moral laws governed by civic institutions (see Evensky, 1993). The idea that economic efficiency requires internalized ethical behavior (broadly defined) is at the core of what is called the "old" institutionalist school of economics (notably in the writings of Thorstein Veblen and John Kenneth Galbraith). In order to incorporate the broad category of ethical norms into a coherent choice theory, norms can be viewed as external constraints on utility-maximization in which individual desires are limited by social imperatives via some implicit social contract. Amartya Sen (1987) uses an analogy from Freudian psychoanalysis to augment this approach by stipulating that individual preference-orderings be potentially reordered by moral meta-preferences. Sen's framework is able to deal with internalized social norms that contradict self-interested preferences such as not purchasing one's preferred brand of athletic shoe because of working conditions in the company's factories. Furthermore, he can explain other non-rational residuals affecting preference ordering such as the meta-preference of nicotine addiction overturning a smoker's rational preference to quit.

This approach captures more of the essentially responsive interior character of ethical norms than rigid exterior constraints. It does not however address the relationship between the interior (subjective, deductive, theoretical, general, prescriptive, etc.) and the exterior (objective, inductive, empirical, specific, descriptive, etc.) that is the crucial ethical process regulating our rationality. Exploring the workings of rationality is a central part of microeconomics but the question of how preferences are formed is left ostensibly untouched. This is because of the fundamental tautology at the heart of the theory of revealed preferences: the same theory explains how and why economic choices are made. Thus, in defining rational preferences as those that are complete and transitive (along with other assumptions and deductive constructs mentioned above), we make an implicit ethical commitment to a specific historical construct effectively excluding many other evolved behaviors. We cannot of course escape our epistemological context but we can at least attempt to avoid conflating the general and the specific. Furthermore, it may even be possible to use economic concepts to enhance biological and philosophical enquiries into the evolutionary origins of ethics. Economists were after all previously called moral philosophers. I propose that reversing the causality in Smith's assumption – examine how the economic environment affects the evolution of internalized ethical behavior – could shed light on how ethical behavior coevolves with the economic environment.

Evolutionary theorists generally see both ethical imperatives and rational thought as evolved characteristics. As such, different evolutionary schools of thought have been attempting to explain them much as they explain other biological processes. Biologists and evolutionary philosophers have studied the evolution of culture, reason, and ethics within the biological context of Darwinian natural selection. They develop many useful insights and even propose well-formulated accounts of how social structure can evolve from individual selection, but, like evolutionary economists (see Alexander Rosenberg, 2000, and numerous contributions by Geoffrey Hodgson and others), they too struggle with the – ethical in my view – relationship between individual and social evolution.

I will briefly describe the main uniting elements of this literature as it directly applies to the structural view of ethics. Much like economics, the debates in evolutionary theory have their roots in the nineteenth century: specifically gradualism versus saltationism (from the Latin for "jump"). They differ on the relative "oomph" (to use McCloskey's vernacular) of continuous and cumulative natural selection versus catastrophic change. The dinosaurs, for example, were better adapted *structurally* to their environment than early mammals but that advantage was catastrophically offset by the *event* of a comet hitting the Yucatan peninsula. If we are to apply evolutionary thought to the social realm, we must explicitly address this structural dualism. This dualism is predicated on nothing less than our rational understanding of our world through the ethical regime that evolved to negotiate between the general and the specific. The late evolutionary theorist and cultural icon Stephen J. Gould articulated his theory of "punctuated equilibrium" as the current iteration of saltationism (also known as catastrophism). He stresses the degree to which specific events destabilize the general structure of evolution by natural selection at a given time.

In *The Selfish Gene*, Richard Dawkins (1976) uses social insects to propose that if our ultimate goal is spreading our genes then organisms would assign positive proportional weights to the welfare of relatives based on the percentage of genes they share: "kin-selection." Edward Wilson (1975, 1978) with Charles Lumsden (Lumsden and Wilson, 1981;

Lumsden, 1983), and Michael Ruse (see especially his fascinating *Taking Darwin Seriously*, 1998), add two types of altruisms: "Reciprocal altruism" uses a game-theoretical approach to articulate the notion that within a community (national, religious, ethnic, intellectual, etc) individuals stand to benefit from delayed reciprocity for their good deeds. This type of altruism is instrumental in the formation of most communities and their institutions and has been extensively discussed. Reciprocal altruism would be an important aspect of Smith's internalized ethical commitments. The residual – altruistic behavior without a potential gain – is sometimes called "hard-core" altruism. Though this form of ethical behavior is mostly unexplored, recognizing its evolutionary character suggests that, like organisms, it is the result of a historical (and thus partially catastrophic) process of selection from random variations. It would follow that, like physiological characteristics, it exhibits many enduring anachronisms, redundancies, parasites, symbiotes, and, like the majority of genetic material in genomes, is mostly *junk*.

In *Genes, Mind, and Culture*, Lumsden and Wilson (1981) put this conceptual apparatus into motion by developing the concept of "epigenetic rules" which are behavioral characteristics and tendencies that are a consequence of natural selection. The concept of causality, for example, is not simply how the world works (Hume, Nietzsche, and Derrida have thoroughly convinced me). It is nevertheless a central part of rationality both in the loftiest halls of academe as well as whenever we cross a busy street. Our ancestors may have evolved this understanding of the world simply because of the selection bias against those who did not appreciate the difference between a cave into which they saw a Saber-tooth tiger enter, and another cave from which they saw another tiger subsequently exit. Similarly, cooperative behavior and altruism evolved because they had some evolutionary advantage. Concepts such as heroism and even sainthood – as the controversial B. F. Skinner pointed out in *Beyond Freedom and Dignity* (1971) – can be seen as an epigenetic rule to offset variants of the free-rider problem that emerge in cases of significant individual costs. In other words, the extra evolutionary costs (and often risks) to the individual behaving altruistically are offset by benefits derived from socially evolved ethical norms to the benefit of society. As a thoroughly dismal scientist, one could view the concept of "just rewards in the afterlife," for example, as a highly successful social adaptation that harnesses the immediate social benefits of altruistic and cooperative behavior in exchange for an uncertain promise of a deferred reward. I will leave it to the reader to decide whether it is a deity who incurs the costs of the reward, or whether they ultimately are paid by society in other forms (a theological Ricardian equivalence). Nevertheless, even though the sanctioned behaviors are defined within a social, political, and economic context, the ethical structure underwriting specific moralities is an evolved structure much like the causal structure in rationality.

Postmodern ethics?!

Harpham loosely defines this elusive concept based on the observation that virtually all its practitioners subscribe to a Nietzschean interpretation of ethics: "a mere fabrication for purposes of gulling: at best, an artistic fiction; at worst, an outrageous imposture" (*Genealogy of Morals* in Harpham, 1995: 389). Consequently, a lot of ink has been spent in what Poovey (1998) calls a "denunciatory mode" in which anything and everything was subjected to deconstructive exposure as politically and thus ethically motivated. Specific social (hence political and economic) institutional arrangements were convincingly shown to depend on the acceptance of metaphysical universal ethical principles.

The strong skepticism regarding ethical discourse that united a generation of critical theorists reached a defining historical impasse in 1987. The influential deconstructive philosopher Paul de Man was exposed on the pages of the *New York Times* as having written a large number of articles for a Belgian collaborationist newspaper in 1941–42. Practitioners of deconstruction, who had hitherto resisted any evaluation of an author – let alone an ethical one – found it impossible to ignore the ensuing criticism and its political implications. The consequent debacle, while often apologetic, has motivated a re-evaluation of the role of ethics in knowledge-production based on the work of Michel Foucault (1966a, 1966b/1970, and 1969/1972). Perhaps best described as a social archeologist, Foucault attempted to uncover the structural regularities in ethics, and thus develop a conceptualization of ethics as a discursive regime that proceeds by imposing binary hierarchical oppositions. These oppositions are ontologically and epistemologically interdependent since the discursive regime bases its hierarchy on claims to otherness. Good, for example, can neither exist, nor be understood without reference to Evil. Since rational inquiry requires negotiating the ontological–epistemological divide to produce a discourse of truth (theological, scientific, or otherwise), ethics follows the old adage by dividing concepts in order to rule their meaning.

6 Peroration

The (lowercase-t) truth about McCloskey

Ethics itself has evolved as a framework solution to problems arising at the intersection between the individual and the social. Among other branches of economics, game theoretical studies of enforcement mechanisms are quite good at exposing these problems. The Prisoner's Dilemma is the most well known example of game theory. It formally tells the story of two prisoners whom the police cannot convict of a major crime based only on evidence. They are arrested, kept apart, and separately offered to cut a deal with the police in exchange for a light sentence. But there's a catch; a prisoner who is betrayed by the other (having *not* confessed himself) will bear the full brunt of the law, while the other goes free. Strategically, betrayal is very attractive because the collaborator will, at worse, receive a medium sentence in jail, and, at best, can hope to *cooperate* with the other prisoner to receive a light sentence. The optimal outcome that is *best for both* is not to collaborate with the police and thus both face a relatively light sentence (the police can convict them for a lesser crime). The story is laid out formally in Table 4.

The dilemma is that, *in the absence of cooperation*, one prisoner cannot trust the other to be silent and thus strict rationality in the absence of ethical institutions such as moral codes would lead them each to confess. They will thus end up in the worse possible outcome for both, which is the non-cooperative one. This non-cooperative solution (called a Nash equilibrium after the economics Nobel laureate mathematician John Nash) is

Table 4 The Prisoner's Dilemma

Strategies available to each prisoner	Prisoner A collaborates with the police and confesses	Prisoner A is silent
Prisoner B collaborates with the police and confesses	*Non-cooperative outcome:* Medium sentence for both	B goes home A rots in jail
Prisoner B is silent	A goes home B rots in jail	*Cooperative outcome:* Light sentence for both

Note
Only one of the four possible outcomes (within the dark frame) actually happens.

worse than the cooperative solution *for both prisoners* but the lack of trust (or other enforcement mechanism) between the prisoners bars them from achieving such a socially optimal outcome for themselves. The historical fact that prisoners tend to adhere to a moral code of silence to solve this famous dilemma is an excellent example of how moral codes evolve in response to an economic environment in which the dilemma is defined in terms of costs and benefits. Behaviors and institutions that are able to avoid the non-cooperative outcome are evolutionarily beneficial.

Natural selection has yielded a patchwork of workable solutions necessary for the rational reconstruction of systematic knowledge from haphazard events. These solutions became increasingly important as language evolved and communication needed to be rationalized into early language communities in which the question "how do you know?" heralded the birth of epistemology. Epistemology was urgently needed in an early human society that depended increasingly on the transfer of knowledge and skills through learning from others. Soon thereafter relatively simple pieces of information must have given way to more complex principles ranging from stone-craft to mysticism. Principles need to be *generally* applicable to a range of *specific* cases and this becomes particularly tricky when applied to the social realm. This amalgam of partial solutions to social problems and conflicts including versions of the prisoner's dilemma *is* ethics. This is an ontology which views ethics as a central component of our evolved capacity for rational thought. Ethical reasoning is the mechanism rational organisms use to escape the evolutionarily counterproductive dogma of unfounded certainty on the one hand, and paralyzing skepticism on the other.

I have been supplementing McCloskey's strong claims for the role of open debate in science with very strong claims as to the central role of ethics in human reasoning. It follows that the *petitio principii* (question begged) raises the fundamental question of the origins of this omnipresent ethical structure. Evolutionary theory – on which much of economic thought is predicated – can supply us with fruitful consiliences of induction. The many applications of evolutionary theory to economics continue to struggle with the old difficulties at the intersection between biological and cultural evolution. I would therefore suggest that an economic understanding of institutions and incentive-systems, augmented by an ethical understanding of knowledge-production as a process of generalizing the specific, could significantly contribute to an understanding of the evolution of the historical context in which we produce economic knowledge. A historical, structural, and skeptical ethics (a critical ethics?) can enhance our understanding of the irreducible multiplicity of our knowledge of the world, and how this affects our economies, academies, and everything in between.

My reading of Hausman and McPherson (1994) is an example of using deconstructive procedures for studying ethics in that they show how a set of metaphysically based beliefs serves as a hidden ethical foundation for both normative and positive economics. This analysis, with several adaptations and extensions, adumbrates McCloskey's metaphysical foundations and the system of exclusions and ethical commitments (explicit and implicit) supporting it (see *Peroration* and *Appendix II*). However, as we have seen, foundations are remarkably durable even if they are suspended in thin air. Furthermore, they are even quite reasonable in a specific context, and perhaps even necessary for any evaluation, prescription, or rational thought for that matter. At the very least in advocating her free-market discourse-ethic, she calls our attention to its rhetoric, dysfunctions, politics, sociology, and ethics. In this sense, McCloskey is very pragmatic in relation to analytically utopian correspondence theories of truth (such as Mäki's or Lawson's) which struggle to maintain a credible connection with an unknowable real world. Consequently, it may be more intellectually productive to examine the social institutions of academe than the structure of their theories.

This is not to say that examining theories cannot be highly productive, especially when done in a rhetorically critical fashion. In fact there is a fascinating parallel tradition almost exactly contemporary with McCloskey and the rhetoric of economics – Radical Subjectivism – that uses many of the arguments at the core of McCloskey's position. Even more pragmatically promising is that these approaches are influential in *politically* diverse economic schools of thought. Austrians other than McCloskey have embraced some form of subjectivism (see *The Economics of Time and Ignorance*, O'Driscoll and Rizzo, 1985), and on the other side of the political spectrum, post-Keynesians have produced philosophically compatible works. While hardly overturning the orthodoxy, these multiple assaults have perhaps at least mollified the status quo in the meta-conversation on economics. Furthermore, the various applications of subjectivist thought in economics have yet to reach their apex.

As things ostensibly stand at the turn of the century, sophisticated realists such as Mäki and Lawson have had the upper hand in their debate with McCloskey and her pomo[1] ilk. This common (but by no means universal) perception depends on the significant misunderstandings and incommensurabilities I have discussed in this text. In my discussion of the Mäki diagnosis, I mentioned that the bone of contention which divides Mäki and McCloskey is that postmodernism holds that there is no such thing as an emancipating and progressive *theory* (or methodology); only emancipating *practices*. Progressive realists such as Mäki are searching for the holy grail of social theory in the form of an analytical theory that would be able to lead to Truth independent of any socio-political bias.

McCloskey's Habermassian discourse ethic (*sprachethik*) obviously falls short. But then again, what doesn't? In a sense, McCloskey is repeating Winston Churchill's famous comment about democracy being the least awful among several terrible options for government. If there is no way of adjudicating truth on purely analytical grounds, isn't it better if the scientific elite's discourse is ethical? Can there be an advantage to excluding certain types of discourse for specific analytical criteria which are themselves also socially constructed by an elite? It would thus be possible to accuse Mäki of elitism along similar ground to those he himself uses against McCloskey (see *Division*).

The crux of the matter is, I believe, that the rhetorical approach highlights the specific exclusions that support the elite instead of hiding them behind analytical constructs. It is much harder to abuse one's discursive power when the discourse ethics are under scrutiny and the elite are seen as such, than when discursive power is assumed to rely on a correspondence with a transcendental but absolute reality. Furthermore, I think Mäki would agree that by viewing specific methodological principles as correspondent with nature (even if indirectly and critically), one opens the door to a particularly hurtful opposition between natural and unnatural. The use of this hierarchical opposition is one of the principal culprits in the exercise of modernist power, and has and still does inflict significant pain on multitudes of people. When one pays attention to rhetoric and studies truth as a social construct, one cannot explain away unemployment or discrimination or any other kind of injustices by calling them *natural*. Finally, it should be noted that McCloskey has voluntarily left the highest echelons of the economics elite when she left the University of Chicago to pursue her agenda to enhance the discourse ethics of economics. She certainly cannot be accused of not practicing what she preaches.

More generally, McCloskey should be credited with stimulating much of the recent interest in applications of modern non-analytical philosophy to economics. Her rhetoric has successfully undermined a major hierarchical opposition supporting the metaphysical system of positivist methodology: substance over form. In doing so, she has joined the ranks of philosophers and scientists, who engage in internal criticism of universal methodological criteria, showing how they fail to fulfill their own criteria. Her prescription of *sprachethik* is a call for enlightened methodological pluralism that few of us would reject but is founded on a norm that is, by definition, a product of exclusion. Her norm is based on a restricted community of economists employing a rhetorical ethic of conversation to produce justified economic truth. She has thus substituted the content/form hierarchical opposition with a different but closely related opposition in her ethics of truth: socially constructed lowercase-t truth over absolute uppercase-T Truth. This, as we have seen, leads directly to the longest and most circular conversation in human history: the realist versus relativist debate, and, for a while, it seemed that McCloskey and her critics had lost their way in that quagmire.

Using a structural approach to ethics to understand McCloskey's enterprise – both her critique of economic methodology and her philosophy of economic rhetoric – shows that she has introduced the opposition with its traditional hierarchy reversed: Lowercase-t truth dominates uppercase-T Truth *ethically* because its pluralism and tolerance is a *contextually* appropriate reference in discourse-ethical scientific conversation. This is a textbook deconstructive move: McCloskey shows the substance/form opposition to be metaphysical or ideological by revealing its presuppositions and showing how it undermines the texts that employ it. Simultaneously she maintains the oppositional structure by employing the traditional Truth/truth opposition in her text, and reverses its hierarchy to see how this would affect its functioning in the texts that employ it and the metaphysical system it supports. McCloskey has done her homework on postmodernism since *Knowledge and Persuasion in Economics* (1994) and fully appreciates that deconstruction is not a theory (let alone an alternative epistemology) but a process and a tool.

McCloskey is now beginning to articulate the bourgeois ethics that she prescribes for economics. In her upcoming four-volume project under the working title of *The Bourgeois Virtues: Ethics for an Age of Capitalism*, she finally addresses the political dimensions of her discourse ethic in a broad historical context. Of course, as we have seen, all discourse is both political and ethical but unlike the traditional *hierarchies* in the transference of philosophical foundations from academe to the soap box, here we have a deconstruction with direct ethical political application. She writes about how ethical sentiments and zeitgeists have been shaping venerated social institutions in realms ranging from fine arts to high finance over the last several centuries. She even develops an intriguing cyclical view of ethics emanating from the interplay of social classes over time.

The rhetoric of economics is crucial because its discourses are a central part of how economic systems evolve as they come under the increasing pressures of globalization. Is it not time to finally drop the post- prefix and call this philosophy *new pragmatism*?

Appendix I
Historical background

In this appendix, I will briefly present the philosophy of language ostensibly espoused by most economists since the 1930s. While abandoned by most philosophers since the 1950s, some form of positivism continues – at least implicitly – to serve as a philosophical foundation for the bulk of economics to this day. Furthermore, most economists no longer bother to seriously contemplate the philosophical foundations or consequences of their work and, when pressed on the matter, resort to embarrassing clichés unworthy of the intellectual sophistication they show in other respects. It is thus worthwhile to spend a little time on positivism and its history in economics in order to provide a context in which to read McCloskey as well as her critics.

The French mathematician and philosopher Auguste Comte developed the system of philosophy referred to today as classical positivism. The idea of knowledge based on experience of natural phenomena is not new as such and can be traced directly to David Hume and the Duc de Saint-Simon, and more indirectly to the general modes of thought that constituted the Scientific Revolution of the seventeenth century. Immanuel Kant should probably also be seen as a predecessor of classical positivism due to his focus on logic and reason and especially his differentiation of modes of thinking into analytic and synthetic propositions – a differentiation that was to become the cornerstone of the positivist position. An analytic proposition is one in which the predicate is contained in the subject, as in the statement "blue skies are blue." The predicate here is the affirmation "is blue" which is directed at the subject "blue skies." Such propositions are called analytic because truth is discovered by the *logical* analysis of the concept itself; to state the reverse would be to make the proposition self-contradictory. Synthetic propositions, on the other hand, are those that cannot be arrived at by pure logical analysis, as in the statement "the sky is blue." All propositions that result from *experience of the world* are by definition synthetic.

Positivism however significantly departs from Kant by rejecting his concept of a priori propositions that, in contrast to synthetic (or empirical) propositions that depend entirely on sense perception, have a fundamental obvious validity, and are not based on such perception. The difference between these two types of proposition may be illustrated by the empirical "the sun moves against the perceived sky" and the a priori "one plus one equals two." In the *Critique of Pure Reason* (1787), Kant views objects of the material world as the raw material from which sensations are formed and thus fundamentally unknowable through reason. Objects, space, and time exist only as part of the mind, as intuitions by which perceptions are measured and synthetic a priori judgments are made.

Like British utilitarianism, Comte was interested in a reorganization of social life for the good of humanity through scientific knowledge and the control of natural forces that such knowledge allows. The two primary components of classical positivism, the philosophy and the polity, were combined by Comte into a religion, in which Humanity was the object of worship. A number of Comte's disciples refused, however, to accept this religious development because it seemed to contradict the original positivist philosophy. Many of Comte's doctrines were later adapted and developed by the social philosophers John Stuart Mill and Herbert Spencer and by the philosopher and physicist Ernst Mach.

Positivism becomes more immediately relevant to economic methodology with its transformation into logical positivism in the 1920s. I will only briefly mention that Positivism was first explicitly introduced into economic methodology in 1938 with the publication of Terence Hutchison's *The Significance and Basic Postulates of Economic Theory*, but the "wholesale-conversion" of the discipline's orthodoxy was only to take place after the world wars.[1] The anti-metaphysical ideals of positivism were addressed and developed as a methodological issue for practicing scientists during Moritz Schlick's evening meetings at the University of Vienna from 1922 to 1933.

Even before it gave birth to logical positivism, the Vienna Circle represented a departure from the classical positivist philosophical tradition in that its participants were not philosophers interested in science but scientists interested in philosophy. This may seem to be a rather trivial point to make but is in fact quite relevant in that it adumbrates the intellectual and political context in which modern methodology developed. The relationship between the sciences and their methods is a central aspect of McCloskey's work. The workings of this relationship will be addressed on several occasions in this text, but at this point I only want to propose that it is far from simple and that it is not symmetrical: An economist who philosophizes on economics engages the issues at hand from a different perspective than a philosopher of science specializing in economics. I would suggest that much of the impasses in debates in the philosophy of economics are due to the social incommensurability of the two perspectives. In other words, philosophers of science and economists-philosophers contextualize the issues differently because they hold very different intellectual and political stakes in the debate. As I will demonstrate repeatedly and from different perspectives in this text, different contexts motivated by different social interests give rise to different interpretations, different meanings, and even different truths.

Bruce Caldwell (1982) sees the move away from positivism as triggered by a shifting of the *scope* of the philosophy of science from the positivist concern with the context of *justification* to the emerging "growth-of-knowledge" philosophers of the 1960s and their inquiries into the context of *discovery*. The first characteristic of the new approaches was their dissatisfaction with an absolute, static, and consequently simplistic view of the *evolution* of theories, and their call for enhanced *descriptive power*. Instead of timeless criteria for what constitutes valid and justified scientific knowledge, these new theorists attempted to produce an account of the historical *events* that shape science, rather than *structures* that govern it. The second characteristic of this shift from static to dynamic meta-theory is the extent to which different variants struggle to enhance the *prescriptive power* of methodology, which depends on the ability to generalize systematic methodological laws from the historical accounts. The skepticism that undermined the epistemological foundations of positivism did not disappear with its demise. Only Imre Lakatos (1970a and b) stands out as having formulated a prescriptive methodological program based on dynamic epistemological foundations. Others – though very successful in criticizing positivism – were only able (or willing) to produce weak prescriptive methodologies (e.g. Thomas Kuhn, 1962) or resorted to abandoning such pursuits entirely (e.g. Paul Feyerabend, 1975).

Imre Lakatos (1970a and b) could be seen as representing the state-of-the-art paradigm for strongly prescriptive methodology in the philosophy of science. The central feature of "sophisticated methodological falsificationism" is its evolutionary view of research traditions as constituted from a dynamic series of theories, which evolve through time and compete with each other over which series is better able to adapt to falsifying evidence that emerges in a fluid scientific environment. These adaptations are accomplished with "problemshifts" which can be seen as mutations in the series of theories that constitute a research program. The implicit evolutionary description of science – though rhetorically convincing – relies on heuristic principles with doubtful descriptive power. Caldwell (1982) has argued that Lakatos's most important divergence from his mentor Sir Karl Popper is that he de-emphasizes refutation by decisive tests and relies entirely on adjudging problemshifts for their progressiveness: the ability to anticipate new facts (theoretically progressive) of which some are corroborated (empirically progressive). This implies that falsification does not necessarily lead to a rejection of a theory unless a ready alternative is available. Lakatos introduced heuristic strategies designed to police the balance of continuity and progress in research programs. This balance is maintained with a "refutable protective belt" within which progressive problemshifts are allowed to carry new information to the refutable variants of the research program while the irrefutable "hard-core" safeguards the continuity of the program.

On the opposing end of the prescriptive–descriptive spectrum from Lakatos among 1970s philosophers of science is Paul Feyerabend. The notorious principle of "anything goes" (1975: 28) emanates from the descriptive observation that anything *has* gone in the past, and there is no reason to believe that prescribing the exclusion of some things from going now will guarantee better science from now on. It is interesting to note that Feyerabend's *carnavalesque* anti-method is the least vague with regard to the description–prescription opposition. This is precisely because his main argument is based on the tension between a historical *description* of the vagaries of scientists' behavior and a *prescription* of an optimal methodological policy. He is essentially offering that given our meager understanding of knowledge production, accumulation, and interpretation, the only reasonable methodological maxim is, "if it isn't broken, don't fix it." Any set of methodological rules are a form of social engineering in that they simplistically interpret, and claim to be able to manipulate, a system whose complexity they cannot even fathom. Caldwell (1982: 225) explains that methodological "canons of choice" proceed by eliminating theories. If facts depend on interpretation, and interpretation depends on specific theoretical presuppositions, it follows that each theory has its specific empirical content, which is lost if the theory is discarded. In this respect, Feyerabend's call for theory proliferation is similar to Caldwell's methodological pluralism. They differ however in the role they give to methodology. Unlike Feyerabend's Dadaist non-prescription, Caldwell prescribes an inquiry based on explicit rational reconstruction and *internal* criticism – criticism from within the theoretical context of the object under investigation.

The most famous philosopher of science is Thomas Kuhn, whose *The Structure of Scientific Revolutions* (1962) has become iconic of the contemporary rise of skepticism in the philosophy and methodology of science. The basis of his theory is the distinction between "normal science" and "revolutionary science," and the concepts according to which the distinction is made: paradigm and paradigm-shift. Normal science is a science that follows the example of previous science and follows the prescriptive framework delineated by the paradigm to which it belongs. Normal science specifically does not problematize aspects of the paradigm and seeks only to extend the received view and, more importantly, perform the pedagogical function of training new scientists in the specific paradigm-lore. In a Lakatosian research program the irrefutable hard-core is protected from even progressive problemshifts by an absolute negative heuristics tied to the entire set of ideas forming the hard-core. In Kuhn's view, there is an *endogenous* mechanism by which the paradigm is protected. I would call it indoctrination-by-doing, a variant of the familiar economic concept of learning-by-doing that is a part of production theory, and refers to the phenomena by which human capital (workers' abilities as means of production) and thus productivity rise with experience. Kuhn, like Lakatos, believed continuity to be paramount and considered this aspect of normal science as beneficial. By founding his paradigms on the concept of socialization, Kuhn significantly softens the Lakatosian hard-core while specifying an underlying mechanism that can be observed and studied.

For Kuhn, a new idea emerges from normal science through a process of accumulating anomalies. The pedantic drive of normal science inevitably discovers and exposes problems and contradictions in the para-digm which, having reached a certain critical mass, result in crisis. If practi-tioners are unable to reconcile the anomalies with the existing paradigm then a revolution ensues in which a new paradigm challenges the incum-bent. The point made in the last sentence is that the symptoms of crisis are in fact attempts at constructing and establishing a new paradigm *not* in order to eliminate normal science but in order to enable normal science to proceed again. The revolutionary prerequisite of an alternative paradigm has two important consequences that challenge both falsificationism and empiricism in general, and the very idea of a single prescriptive methodol-ogy. First, theories are accepted or rejected based not only on inconsisten-cies with data, but also on a comparison with *other theories* and their structural position within their paradigm. Second, Kuhn specifically asserts that with a change in paradigm come not only changes in predictions, descriptions, and explanations but also changes in method and domain, which are the basis of the positivist distinction between scientific (enlight-ened) and metaphysical (superstitious) knowledge. "The normal-scientific tradition that emerges from a scientific revolution is not only incompatible but often actually incommensurable with that which has gone before" (Kuhn, 1970: 103). Herein lay the seeds of the social-constructivist para-digm in contemporary philosophy of science. If standards and criteria for theory choice are contextually tied to a specific paradigm, a scientific revolution renders these standards obsolete. It follows therefore there is no single methodology that will ensure progress towards the truth no mater how broadly the latter is defined.

McCloskey subscribes to Kuhn's skepticism but adds several new dimensions to it. There is the fundamental recognition that economics is itself constituted from words embedded in texts that are based on common language yet, at the same time, those same texts are constantly intervening and re-defining the language in an attempt to control its ambiguities. McCloskey goes to literary and linguistic theory in an attempt to illumi-nate these issues and I follow her there.

Appendix II

The ethical strata in economic theory

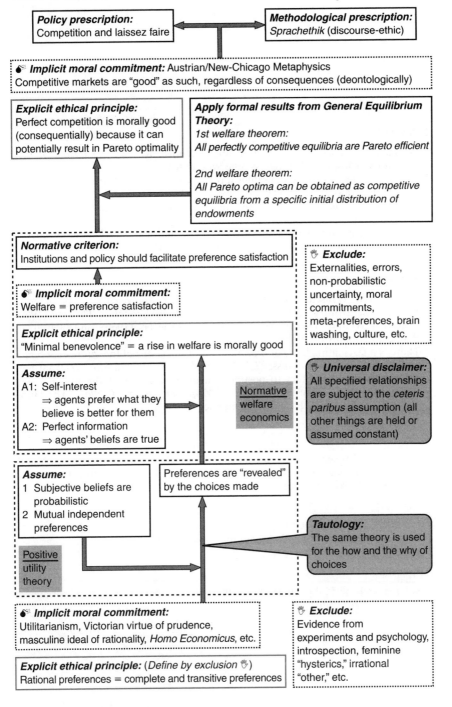

Policy prescription:
Competition and laissez faire

Methodological prescription:
Sprachethik (discourse-ethic)

☝ **Implicit moral commitment:** Austrian/New-Chicago Metaphysics
Competitive markets are "good" as such, regardless of consequences (deontologically)

Explicit ethical principle:
Perfect competition is morally good (consequentially) because it can potentially result in Pareto optimality

Apply formal results from General Equilibrium Theory:
1st welfare theorem:
All perfectly competitive equilibria are Pareto efficient

2nd welfare theorem:
All Pareto optima can be obtained as competitive equilibria from a specific initial distribution of endowments

Normative criterion:
Institutions and policy should facilitate preference satisfaction

☝ **Implicit moral commitment:**
Welfare ≡ preference satisfaction

Explicit ethical principle:
"Minimal benevolence" ≡ a rise in welfare is morally good

Assume:
A1: Self-interest
⇒ agents prefer what they believe is better for them
A2: Perfect information
⇒ agents' beliefs are true

Normative welfare economics

☝ **Exclude:**
Externalities, errors, non-probabilistic uncertainty, moral commitments, meta-preferences, brain washing, culture, etc.

☝ **Universal disclaimer:**
All specified relationships are subject to the *ceteris paribus* assumption (all other things are held or assumed constant)

Assume:
1 Subjective beliefs are probabilistic
2 Mutual independent preferences

Preferences are "revealed" by the choices made

Tautology:
The same theory is used for the how and the why of choices

Positive utility theory

☝ **Implicit moral commitment:**
Utilitarianism, Victorian virtue of prudence, masculine ideal of rationality, *Homo Economicus*, etc.

☝ **Exclude:**
Evidence from experiments and psychology, introspection, feminine "hysterics," irrational "other," etc.

Explicit ethical principle: (*Define by exclusion* ☝)
Rational preferences ≡ complete and transitive preferences

Notes

2 Narration

1 All page references in this section are to *Knowledge and Persuasion in Economics* (McCloskey, 1994) unless otherwise noted.
2 When available, I give bibliographical references to both the original French and the English translations of Derrida's works.
3 McCloskey omits point number five from her Mirowski quote that I reproduce in its entirety.
4 Surveys are no longer even considered to be empirical data for the purpose of National Endowment for the Sciences (US) grants (!?!).

3 Division

1 See Vincent Tarascio's, *Pareto's Methodological Approach to Economics: A Study in the History of Some Scientific Aspects of Economic Thought* (1968), "Paretian Welfare Theory: Some Neglected Aspects" (1969), and "Pareto on Political Economy" (1974).
2 There is a fascinating body of literature about the status of the gift in economics. Best known is Marcel Mauss, "*Essai sur le don*" (1925), but more relevant here are recent works relating to postmodern interpretations of the gift including Philip Mirowski, "Refusing the Gift" (2001), and Antonio Callari, "The Ghost of the Gift: The Unlikelihood of Economics" (2002).

4 Proof

1 The title of this section comes from the title of McCloskey's response to Mäki's diagnosis (see page 63): "Modern Epistemology Against Analytical Philosophy: A Reply to Mäki" (McCloskey, 1995a: 1319–23).

6 Peroration

1 Pomo is a short term of endearment for postmodernism.

Appendix 1

1 See research by Philip Mirowski on the military operations-research origins of neoclassical economics.

Bibliography

Archer, M., Bhaskar, R., Collier, A., Lawson, T., and Norrie, A. (eds) (1998) *Critical Realism: Essential Readings*, London: Routledge.

Aune, J. A. (2001) *Selling the Free Market: The Rhetoric Of Economic Correctness*, New York: Guilford Press.

Austin, J. (1962) *How to Do Things with Words*, Cambridge, MA: Harvard University Press.

Ayer, A. J. (1936, 1946) *Language, Truth and Logic*, London: V. Gollancz.

—— (ed.) (1959) *Logical Positivism*, Glencoe, IL: Free Press.

Backhouse, R. E. (ed.) (1994) *New Directions in Economic Methodology*, London: Routledge.

—— (1997) *Truth and Progress in Economic Knowledge*, Cheltenham, UK; Lyme, NH: Edward Elgar.

Balak, B. (2000) "The Growth of Knowledge and the Meta-Narratives of Scientific Evolution," presented at the History of Economics Society's 27th annual meeting at the University of British Columbia, Vancouver, June.

Barthes, R. (1977) *Image, Music, Text*, New York: Hill and Wang.

Bellofiore, R. (1994) "The Poverty of Rhetoric: Keynes versus McCloskey," in A. Marzola and F. Silva (eds) *John Maynard Keynes: Language and Method*, Aldershot, Hants, UK; Brookfield, VT: Edward Elgar.

Bhaskar, R. (1975, 1997) *A Realist Theory of Science*, London: Verso.

—— (1989) *Reclaiming Reality*, London: Verso.

—— (1998) "General Introduction," in M. Archer, R. Bhaskar, A. Collier, T. Lawson, and A. Norrie (eds) *Critical Realism: Essential Readings*, London: Routledge.

Blaug, M. (1985) *Economic Theory in Retrospect* (4th edn), Cambridge, UK; New York: Cambridge University Press

Bloom, H., de Man, P., Derrida, J., Hartman, G., and Hillis Miller, J. (eds) (1979) *Deconstruction and Criticism*, New York: Seabury Press.

Brock, W. A. (1988) "Introduction to Chaos and Other Aspects of Nonlinearity," in W. A. Brock and A. G. Malliaris (eds) *Differential Equations, Stability, and Chaos in Dynamic Economics*, New York: Elsevier Science Publishing Company.

Brodbeck, M. and Feigl, H. (eds) (1953) *Readings in the Philosophy of Science*, New York: Appleton-Century-Crofts.

Broody, B. (ed.) (1970) *Readings in the Philosophy of Science*, Englewood Cliffs, NJ: Prentice-Hall.

Buck, R. and Cohen, R. (eds) (1970) *S.A. 1970: In Memory of Rudolf Carnap.* *Boston Studies in the Philosophy of Science*, Vol. VIII, Dordrecht, Netherlands: D. Reidel Publishing Company.

Caldwell, B. J. (1982, 1994) *Beyond Positivism: Economic Methodology in the 20th Century*, London; New York: Routledge.

Callari, A. (2002) "The Ghost of the Gift: The Unlikelihood of Economics," in Mark Osteen (ed.) *The Question of the Gift*, London: Routledge.

Carnap, R. (1934, 1937) *The Logical Syntax of Language*, London: K. Paul, Trench, Trubner & Co.

—— (1942) *Introduction to Semantics*, Cambridge, MA: Harvard University Press.

—— (1947) *Meaning and Necessity: A Study in Semantics and Modal Logic*, Chicago, IL: University of Chicago Press.

—— (1959) "The Elimination of Metaphysics through Logical Analysis of Language," in A. J. Ayer (ed.) *Logical Positivism*, Glencoe, IL: Free Press.

Coats, A. W. (1987) "Comment on McCloskey," *Eastern Economic Journal*, 13.

Collier, A. (1994) *Critical Realism: An Introduction to Roy Bhaskar's Philosophy*, London: Verso.

Comte, A. (1995) *Système de politique positive ou Traité de sociologie instituant la religion de l'humanité.* Available online at: http://www.Gallica.bnf.fr., Bibliothèque National de France, electronic document server reference: Num. BNF de l'éd. de, Osnabrück: O. Zeller, 1967. 23 cmFac-sim. de l'éd. de, [S.I.] : [s.n.], 1851–1881 (République occidentale), (accessed 17 June 2005).

Cullenberg, S., Amariglio, J., and Ruccio, D. F. (eds) (2001) *Postmodermism, Economics and Knowledge*, London: Routledge.

Culler, J. (1982) *On Deconstruction*, Ithaca, NY: Cornell University Press.

Davis, J. B., Hands, W. D., and Mäki, U. (eds) (1998) *The Handbook of Economic Methodology*, Cheltenham, UK; Northampton, MA: Edward Elgar.

Dawkins, R. (1976) *The Selfish Gene*, Oxford, UK: Oxford University Press.

Deleuze, G. (1986, 1988) *Foucault*, Minneapolis: University of Minnesota Press.

Derrida, J. (1967/1978) *L'Ecriture et la différence*, English translation: *Writing and Difference*, Chicago, IL: University of Chicago Press.

—— (1972/1981) *Positions*, Chicago, IL: University of Chicago Press.

—— (1976) *Of Grammatology*, translated from *De la grammatologie* (1967), Baltimore, MD: Johns Hopkins University Press.

—— (1977a) "Signature Event Context," in *Glyph*, 1, translated from *Marges de la philosophie* (1972).

—— (1977b) "Limited Inc a b c," *Glyph*, 2.

—— (1978/1979) "Le Parergon," in *La Vérité en peinture*, English translation: "The Parergon," in *October*, 9, 3–40.

—— (1979) "Living On: Border Lines," in Bloom, 1979, 81.

—— (1980/1978) "Spéculer – 'Sur Freud'," in *La Carte postale: De Socrate à Freud et au-delà*, English translation: "Speculating – On Freud," *Oxford Literary Review*, 3, 78–97.

—— (1981) *Dissemination*, translated from *La Dissémination* (1972), Chicago, IL: University of Chicago Press.

—— (1988) *Limited Inc.*, Graff Gerald (ed.) a collection including *Signature Event Context*, "Limited Inc a b c," and "Afterword: Toward an Ethic of Discussion," Evanston, IL: Northwestern University Press.

—— (1995) *Archive Fever: A Freudian Impression*, Chicago, IL; London: University of Chicago Press.

Eagleton, T. (1976) *Marxism and Literary Criticism*, Berkeley, CA: University of California Press.

—— (1983) *Literary Theory: An Introduction*, Minneapolis, MN: University of Minnesota Press.

Eco, U. (1981) *The Role of the Reader: Explorations in the Semiotics of Texts*, Bloomington, IN: Indiana University Press.

—— (1995) *The Search for the Perfect Language*, Oxford, UK; Cambridge, MA: Blackwell.

—— (1998) *Serendipities: Language and Lunacy*, New York: Columbia University Press.

Evensky, J. (1993) "Ethics and the Invisible Hand," *Journal of Economic Perspectives*, 7, 2, 197–205.

Fernández, R. G. (1999) "McCloskey and Mäki on Truth," paper presented at the History of Economics Society 26th annual meeting in Greensboro, NC.

Feyerabend, P. K. (1970a) "How To Be a Good Empiricist – A Plea for Tolerance in Matters Epistemological," in B. Broody (ed.) *Readings in the Philosophy of Science*, Englewood Cliffs, NJ: Prentice-Hall.

—— (1970b) "Consolations for the Specialist," in I. Lakatos and A. Musgrave (eds) *Criticism and the Growth of Knowledge*, Cambridge, UK; New York: Cambridge University Press.

—— (1975) *Against Method: Outline of an Anarchist Theory of Knowledge*, London: NLB; Atlantic Highlands: Humanities Press.

—— (1999) *Conquest of Abundance: A Tale of Abstraction versus the Richness of Being*, Terpstra Bert (ed.) Chicago, IL: University of Chicago Press.

Fish, S. (1980) *Is There a Text in This Class? The Authority of Interpretive Communities*, Cambridge, MA: Harvard University Press.

Foucault, M. (1966a) "La pensée du dehors," *Critique*, 229, 523–46, June.

—— (1966b/1970) *Les mots et les choses*, English translation: *The Order of Things: An Archaeology of the Human Sciences*, London: Tavistock Publications.

—— (1969/1972) *L'archéologie du savoir*, English translation: *The Archaeology of Knowledge*, New York: Pantheon Books.

—— (1972/1973) *Naissance de la clinique* (earlier version, 1963), English translation: *The Birth of the Clinic: An Archaeology of Medical Perception*, New York: Pantheon Books.

—— (1973/1983) *Ceci n'est pas une pipe*, English translation: *This is not a Pipe*, Berkeley, CA: University of California Press.

—— (1975/1977) *Surveiller et punir. Naissance de la prison*, English translation: *Discipline and Punish: The Birth of the Prison*, New York: Pantheon Books.

—— (1976a) "Two Lectures," lecture 2, 93, in D. Hoy (ed.) *Foucault: A Critical Reader*, Oxford, UK; New York: Basil Blackwell.

—— (1976b) *La volonté de savoir (Histoire de la sexualité I)*, Paris: Gallimard, English translation: *The History of Sexuality, vol. 1: An Introduction*, Harmondsworth, Penguin.

—— (1984) *L'usage des plaisirs (Histoire de la sexualité II)*, Paris: Gallimard.

Freud, S. (1919) "The Uncanny," in *Complete Psychological Works* (1953–74).

—— (1953–74) *Complete Psychological Works*, edited by James Strachey, London: Hogarth Press.

Friedman, M. (1953) *Essays in Positive Economics*, Chicago, IL: Chicago University Press.

Fullbrook, E. (ed.) (2002) *Intersubjectivity in Economics: Agents and Structures*, London; New York: Routledge.

Galbraith, J. K. (1973) *Economics and the Public Purpose*, Boston, MA: Houghton Mifflin.

George, D. (2001) *Preference Pollution: How Markets Create the Desires We Dislike*, Ann Arbor, Michigan, MI: University of Michigan Press.

Gibbard, A. and Varian, H. R. (1979) "Economic Models," *Journal of Philosophy*, 75.

Gross, A. G. (1990, 1996) *The Rhetoric of Science*, Cambridge, MA; London, UK: Harvard University Press.

Harpham, G. G. (1992) *Getting It Right: Language, Literature, and Ethics*, Chicago, IL: University of Chicago Press.

—— (1995) "Ethics," in F. Lentricchia and T. McLaughlin (eds) *Critical Terms for Literary Study*, Chicago, IL; London: University of Chicago Press.

Harré, R. (1986) *Varieties of Realism: A Rational for the Natural Sciences*, Oxford: Basil Blackwell.

Hausman, D. M. (ed.) (1984, 1994) *The Philosophy of Economics: An Anthology*, Cambridge, UK; New York: Cambridge University Press.

Hausman, D. and McPherson, M. (1993) "Taking Ethics Seriously: Economics and Contemporary Moral Philosophy," *Journal of Economic Literature*, 31, 671–731.

—— (1994) "Economics, rationality, and ethics," in D. M. Hausman (ed.) *The Philosophy of Economics: An Anthology*, Cambridge, UK; New York: Cambridge University Press.

—— (1996) *Economic Analysis and Moral Philosophy*, Cambridge, UK; New York: Cambridge University Press.

Hawthorn, J. (1992) *A Concise Glossary of Contemporary Literary Theory*, London; New York: Edward Arnold.

Hayek, F. A. (1942–44) "Scientism and the Study of Society," *Economica* (reprinted in *The Counter-Revolution of Science*), Indianapolis, IN: Liberty Press.

Hempel, C. G. (1959) "The Empiricist Criterion of Meaning," in A. J. Ayer (ed.) *Logical Positivism*, Glencoe, IL: Free Press.

Hempel, C. and Oppenheim, P. (1948) "Studies in the Logic of Explanation," *Philosophy of Science*, 15, in M. Brodbeck and H. Feigl (eds) *Readings in the Philosophy of Science*, New York: Appleton-Century-Crofts.

Henderson, W., Dudley-Evans, T., and Backhouse, R. (eds) (1993) *Economics and Language*, London: Routledge.

Hesse, M. (1980) *Revolutions and Reconstructions in the Philosophy of Science*, Bloomington, IN: Indiana University Press.

Horwich, P. (ed.) (1993) *World Changes: Thomas Kuhn and the Nature of Science*, Cambridge, MA; London: MIT Press (a Bradford book).

Hoy, D. (ed.) (1986) *Foucault: A Critical Reader*, Oxford, UK; New York: Basil Blackwell.

Hume, D. (1739–40) *A Treatise of Human Nature: Being an Attempt to introduce the experimental Method of Reasoning into Moral Subjects*. Available online at: http://panoramix.univ-paris1.fr/CHPE/Textes/Hume/treat0.html.

—— (1748) *An Inquiry Concerning Human Understanding*. Available online at: http://www.ecn.bris.ac.uk/het/hume/enquiry.

Hutchison, T. (1938, 1965) *The Significance and Basic Postulates of Economic Theory*, New York: A. M. Kelley, Bookseller.

—— (1992) *Changing Aims in Economics*, Oxford, UK; Cambridge, MA: Basil Blackwell.

Ihde, D. (1993) *Postphenomenology: Essays in the Postmodern Context*, Evanston, IL: Northwestern University Press.

Johnson, B. (1980) "Nothing Fails like Success," *SCE Reports*, 8, 7–16.

Kant, I. (1787, 1964) *Critique of Pure Reason*, London: Macmillan.

—— (1965, *c.*1929) *Critique of Pure Reason*, translated by Norman Kemp Smith, New York: St Martin's Press.

Keynes, J. M. (1936) *The General Theory of Employment, Interest and Money*, London: Macmillan.

Kincaid, H. (1996) *Philosophical Foundations of the Social Sciences: Analyzing Controversies in Social Research*, Cambridge, UK; New York: Cambridge University Press.

Kitcher, P. (1981) "Explanatory Unification," *Philosophy of Science*, 48, 507–31.

Klamer, A. and Colander, D. (1990) *The Making of an Economist*, Boulder, CO: Westview Press.

Klamer, A., McCloskey, D., and Solow, R. (eds) (1988) *The Consequences of Economic Rhetoric*, Cambridge, UK; New York: Cambridge University Press.

Klein, L. (1985) *Economic Theory and Econometrics*, edited by Jaime Marquez, London: Basil Blackwell.

Klein, L. R. (1953) *A Textbook of Econometrics*, Evanston, IL: Row, Peterson.

Kuhn, T. (1962, 1996) *The Structure of Scientific Revolutions*, Chicago, IL; London: University of Chicago Press.

—— (1970) "Reflections on My Critics," in I. Lakatos and A. Musgrave (eds) *Criticism and the Growth of Knowledge*, Cambridge, UK; New York: Cambridge University Press.

Lakatos, I. (1970a) "History of Science and Its Rational Reconstruction," in R. Buck and R. Cohen (eds.) *S.A. 1970: In Memory of Rudolf Carnap. Boston Studies in the Philosophy of Science*, Vol. VIII, Dordrecht, Netherlands: D. Reidel Publishing Company.

—— (1970b) "Falsification and the Methodology of Scientific Research Programmes," in I. Lakatos and A. Musgrave (eds) *Criticism and the Growth of Knowledge*, Cambridge, UK; New York: Cambridge University Press.

Lakatos, I. and Musgrave, A. (eds) (1970) *Criticism and the Growth of Knowledge*, Cambridge, UK; New York: Cambridge University Press.

Lanham, R. (1991) *A Handlist of Rhetorical Terms*, Berkeley; Los Angeles: University of California Press.

Latour, B. (1984, 1988) *The Pasteurization of France*, Cambridge, MA; London: Harvard University Press.

—— (1987) *Science in Action*, Cambridge, MA; London: Harvard University Press.

—— (1999) *Pandora's Hope: Essays on the Reality of Science Studies*, Cambridge, MA; London: Harvard University Press.

Latour, B. and Woolgar, S. (1979) *Laboratory Life. The Social Construction of Scientific Facts*, Beverly Hills, CA: Sage Publications.

Lavoie, D. C. (ed.) (1990) *Economics and Hermeneutics*, London; New York: Routledge & Kegan Paul.

Lawson, T. (1997) *Economics and Reality*, London; New York: Routledge.

Lentricchia, F. and McLaughlin, T. (eds) (1990, 1995) *Critical Terms for Literary Study*, Chicago, IL; London: University of Chicago Press.

Lucas, R. E. (1976) "Econometric Policy Evaluation: A Critique," in K. Brunner and A. H. Meltzer (eds) *The Philips Curve and Labor Markets*, supplement to the *Journal of Monetary Economics*, 19–46.

Lumsden, C. J. (1983) *Promethean Fire: Reflections on the Origin of Mind*, Cambridge, MA: Harvard University Press.

—— and Wilson, E. O. (1981) *Genes, Mind, and Culture*, Cambridge, MA: Harvard University Press.

McCawley, J. D. (1990) "The Dark side of Reason [Review of Feyerabend's Farewell to Reason]," *Critical Review*, 4 (3, Summer): 377–85.

McCloskey, D. (1983) "The Rhetoric of Economics," *Journal of Economic Literature*, 21, 481–517.

—— (1985, 1998) *The Rhetoric of Economics*, Madison, WI: University of Wisconsin Press.

—— (1988a) "The Consequences of Rhetoric," in A. Klamer, D. McCloskey, and R. Solow (eds) *The Consequences of Economic Rhetoric*, Cambridge, UK; New York: Cambridge University Press.

—— (1988b) "Two Replies and a Dialogue on the Rhetoric of Economics: Mäki, Rappaport, and Rosenberg," *Journal of Economics and Philosophy*, 4, 1, 150–66.

—— (1988c) "Thick and Thin Methodologies in the History of Economic Thought," in N. de Marchi (ed.) *The Popperian Legacy in Economics*, Cambridge, UK: Cambridge University Press.

—— (1988d) "The Limits of Expertise: If You're So Smart, Why Ain't You Rich?" *American Scholar*, 57, 393–406.

—— (1989a) "The Very Idea of Epistemology: Comment," *Journal of Economics and Philosophy*, 5, 1, 1–6.

—— (1989b) "Why I Am No Longer a Positivist," *Review of Social Economics*, 47, 3, 225–38.

—— (1990) *If You're So Smart: The Narrative of Economic Expertise*, Chicago: University of Chicago Press.

—— (1991) "Economic Science: A Search Through the Hyperspace of Assumptions?" *Methodus*, 3, 1, 6–16.

—— (1992) McCloskey's commentary on Mirowski, Philip, "Three Vignettes in the State of Economic Rhetoric," in N. de Marchi (ed.) *Post-Popperian Methodology of Economics: Recovering Practice*, Boston, MA: Kluwer Academic Publishers.

—— (1994) *Knowledge and Persuasion in Economics*, Cambridge, UK; New York: Cambridge University Press.

—— (1995a) "Modern Epistemology Against Analytical Philosophy: A Reply to Mäki," *Journal of Economic Literature*, 33, 3, 1319–23.

—— (1995b) "The Insignificance of Statistical Significance," *Scientific American*, April, 32–3.

—— (1995c) "Computation Outstrips Analysis," *Scientific American*, July, 26.

—— (1996) *The Vices of Economists – The Virtues of the Bourgeoisie*, Amsterdam: Amsterdam University Press.

—— (1999) "Cassandra's Open Letter to her Economist Colleagues," in "Other Things Equal" regular column in the *Eastern Economic Journal*, 25, 3, 357–63.

Machlup, F. (1963) *Essays on Economic Semantics*, Englewood Cliffs, NJ: Prentice-Hall.

—— (1978) *Methodology of Economics and other Social Sciences*, New York: Academic Press.

McPherson, M. S. (1984) "Limits on Self-seeking: The Role of Morality in Economic Life," in David Colander (ed.) *Neoclassical Political Economy*, Boston, MA: Ballinger Press.

Mäki, U. (1988a) "How to Combine Rhetoric and Realism in the Methodology of Economics," *Journal of Economics and Philosophy*, 4, 1, 89–109.

—— (1988b) "Realism, Economics, and Rhetoric: A Rejoinder to McCloskey," *Journal of Economics and Philosophy*, 4, 1, 167–9.

—— (1992) "Social Conditioning of Economics," (see also commentary by A. W. Coats), in N. de Marchi (ed.) *Post-Popperian Methodology of Economics: Recovering Practice*, Boston, MA: Kluwer Academic Publishers.

—— (1993) "Two Philosophies of the Rhetoric of Economics," in W. Henderson, T. Dudley-Evans, and R. Backhouse (eds) *Economics and Language*, London: Routledge.

—— (1995) "Diagnosing McCloskey," *Journal of Economic Literature*, 33, 3, 1300–18.

Mäki, U., Gustafsson, B., and Knudsen, C. (eds) (1993) *Rationality, Institutions and Economic Methodology*, London: Routledge.

de Marchi, N. (ed.) (1988) *The Popperian Legacy in Economics*, Cambridge, UK: Cambridge University Press.

—— (ed.) (1992) *Post-Popperian Methodology of Economics: Recovering Practice*, Boston, MA: Kluwer Academic Publishers.

Marzola, A. and Silva, F. (eds) (1994) *John Maynard Keynes: Language and Method*, Aldershot, Hants, UK; Brookfield, VT: Edward Elgar.

Mauss, M. (1925, 1990) *Essai sur le don*, translated by W. D. Halls, *The Gift: The Form and Reason for Exchange in Archaic Societies*, New York: W. W. Norton.

Mirowski, P. (1988) "Shall I Compare Thee to a Minkowski–Ricardo–Leontief–Metzler Matrix of the Mosak–Hicks Type?" in A. Klamer, D. McCloskey, and R. Solow (eds) *The Consequences of Economic Rhetoric*, Cambridge, UK; New York: Cambridge University Press.

—— (1989) *More Heat than Light*, New York: Cambridge University Press.

—— (1990) "The Philosophical Bases of Institutional Economics," in D. C. Lavoie (ed.) *Economics and Hermeneutics*, London; New York: Routledge & Kegan Paul.

—— (1992) "Three Vignettes on the State of Economic Rhetoric", in N. de Marchi (ed.) *Post-Popperian Methodology of Economics: Recovering Practice*, Boston, MA: Kluwer Academic Publishers.

—— (2000) "The Good, the Bad, and the Bungly," *Journal of the History of Economic Thought*, 22, 1, 85–91.

—— (2001) "Refusing the Gift," in S. Collenberg, J. Amariglio, and D. Ruccio (eds) *Postmodernism Economics and Knowledge*, London; New York: Routledge.

Morley, J. (1993) "Defining Postmodernism: Postmodernism seen as the Reversal of Modernist Individuality," *The Electronic Labyrinth* (© 1993–2000 Keep,

McLaughlin, Parmar), University of Virginia. Available online at: http://www.iath.virginia.edu/elab/hfl0242.html (accessed 17 June 2005).

Nietzsche, F. W. (1964, 1995) *The Complete Works of Friedrich Nietzsche*, Stanford, CA: Stanford University Press.

O'Driscoll, G. P. Jr. and Rizzo, M. J. (1985) *The Economics of Time and Ignorance*, Oxford; New York: Basil Blackwell.

O'Neill, J. (1998) "Rhetoric, Science and Philosophy," *Philosophy of the Social Sciences*, 28, 2, 205–25.

Oxford English Dictionary (2nd edn) (2002) CD-ROM, Oxford: Oxford University Press.

Pareto, V. (1963, *c.*1935) *The Mind and Society: A Treatise on General Sociology*, Arthur Livingston (ed.) translation of *Trattato di sociologia generale* (1916) by Andrew Bongiorno and Arthur Livingston, New York: Dover Publications.

Pojam, L. (ed.) (1993) *The Theory of Knowledge: Classical and Contemporary Readings*, Belmont, CA: Wadsworth Publishing.

Poovey, M. (1998) *A History of The Modern Fact: Problems of Knowledge in the Sciences of Wealth and Society*, Chicago, IL; London: University of Chicago Press.

Popper, K. (1934, 1959) *The Logic of Scientific Discovery*, New York: Basic Books.

—— (1970) "Normal Science and its Dangers," in I. Lakatos and A. Musgrave (eds) *Criticism and the Growth of Knowledge*, Cambridge, UK; New York: Cambridge University Press.

—— (1972) *Objective Knowledge: An Evolutionary Approach*, Oxford, UK: Clarendon Press.

Putnam, H. (1990) *Realism with a Human Face*, Cambridge, MA: Harvard University Press.

Queneau, R. (1947) *Exercices de style*, Paris: Gallimard (Folio).

Rorty, R. (1978) "Philosophy as a Kind of Writing: An Essay on Derrida," *New Literary History*, 10, 141–60.

—— (1980) *Philosophy and the Mirror of Nature*, Princeton, NJ: Princeton University Press.

Rosenberg, A. (1988a) "Economics is too Important to be Left to the Rhetoricians," *Economics and Philosophy*, April, 4, 1, 129–49.

—— (1988b) "Rhetoric is Not Important Enough for Economists to Bother About," *Economics and Philosophy*, April, 4, 1, 129–49.

—— (2000) *Darwinism in Philosophy, Social Science and Policy*, Cambridge, UK; New York: Cambridge University Press.

Rossetti, J. (1990) "Deconstructing Robert Lucas", in W. J. Samuels (ed.) *Economics as Discourse: An Analysis of the Language of Economics*, Boston, MA: Kluwer Academic Publishers.

—— (1992) updated and revised version of "Deconstructing Robert Lucas," in N. de Marchi (ed.) *Post-Popperian Methodology of Economics: Recovering Practice*, Boston, MA: Kluwer Academic Publishers.

Rozeboom, W. (1967) "Why I Know So Much More Than You Do," in L. Pojam (ed.) *The Theory of Knowledge: Classical and Contemporary Readings*, Belmont, CA: Wadsworth Publishing. Originally appeared in the *American Philosophy Quarterly*, 1967, 4, 281–90.

Ruse, M. (1975) "Charles Darwin's Theory of Evolution: An Analysis," *Journal of the History of Biology*, 8, 219–41.

—— (1998) *Taking Darwin Seriously: A Naturalistic Approach to Philosophy*, New York: Prometheus Books.

Russell, B. and Whitehead, A. N. (1910–13) *Principia Mathematica*, Cambridge, UK; New York: Cambridge University Press.

Samuels, W. J. (ed.) (1990) *Economics as Discourse: An Analysis of the Language of Economics*, Boston, MA: Kluwer Academic Publishers.

Samuelson, P. (1947) *Foundations of Economic Analysis*, Cambridge, MA: Harvard University Press.

de Saussure, F. (1907, 1960) *Cours de linguistique génerale*, London: Peter Owen.

Searle, J. R. (1970) *Speech Acts: An Essay in the Philosophy of Language*, Cambridge, UK: New York: Cambridge University Press.

—— (1977) "Reiterating the Differences: A Reply to Derrida," *Glyph*, 1, 198–208.

Sen, A. (1973) *On Economic Inequality*, Oxford: Clarendon Press.

—— (1987) *On Ethics and Economics*, Oxford, UK: Basil Blackwell.

Schlick, M. (1959) "Positivism and Realism," in A. J. Ayer (ed.) *Logical Positivism*, Glencoe, IL: Free Press.

Schumpeter, J. A. (1954) *History of Economic Analysis*, New York: Oxford University Press.

—— (1967) *Economic Doctrine and Method: An Historical Sketch*, New York: Oxford University Press (a Galaxy Book).

Skinner, B. F. (1971) *Beyond Freedom and Dignity* (1st edn), New York: Knopf.

Smith, A. (1799) *An Inquiry into the Nature and Causes of the Wealth of Nations* (9th edn.), London: Printed for A. Strahan, and T. Cadell Jun. and W. Davies.

—— (1801) *The Theory of Moral Sentiments; Or, an Essay Towards an Analysis of the Principles by Which Men Naturally Judge Concerning The Conduct and Character, First of Their Neighbours, and Afterwards of Themselves. To Which is Added, a Dissertation on the Origin of Languages* (9th edn.), London: Printed by A. Strahan, for T. Cadell and others.

—— (1978) *Lectures on Jurisprudence*, R. L. Meek, D. D. Raphael, and P. G. Stein (eds), Oxford: Clarendon Press.

Sofianou, E. (1995) "Post-modernism and the Notion of Rationality in Economics," *Cambridge Journal of Economics*, 19, 373–89.

Sokal, A. D. (1996) "Transgressing the Boundaries: Towards a Transformative Hermeneutics of Quantum Gravity," *Social Text*, 46/47, 217–52.

Sokal, A. D. and Bricmont, J. (1997) *Impostures intellectuelles*, Paris: Odile Jacob.

—— (1997, 1998) *Impostures intellectuelles*, Paris: Odile Jacob, trans. *Fashionable Nonsense: Postmodern Intellectuals' Abuse of Science*, New York: Picador.

Solow, R. (1988) "Comments from Inside Economics," in A. Klamer, D. McCloskey, and R. Solow (eds) *The Consequences of Economic Rhetoric*, Cambridge, UK; New York: Cambridge University Press.

Sraffa, P. (1960) *Production of Commodities by Means of Commodities: Prelude to a Critique of Political Economy*, Cambridge, UK: Cambridge University Press.

Stettler, M. (1995) "The Rhetoric of McCloskey's Rhetoric of Economics," *Cambridge Journal of Economics*, 19, 391–403.

Tarascio, V. (1968) *Pareto's Methodological Approach to Economics: A Study in the History of Some Scientific Aspects of Economic Thought*, Chapel Hill, NC: University of North Carolina Press.

—— (1969) "Paretian Welfare Theory: Some Neglected Aspects," *Journal of Political Economy*, 77, 1, 1–20.

—— (1974) "Pareto on Political Economy," *History of Political Economy*, 6, 361–80.

—— (1975) "Intellectual History and the Social Sciences: The Problem of Methodological Pluralism", *Social Science Quarterly*, 55.

—— (1997) "The Problem of Knowledge in Economics," *Southern Economic Journal*, 64, 1.

Tarascio, V. and Caldwell, B. (1979) "Theory-Choice in Economics: Philosophy and Practice," *Journal of Economic Issues*, 13, 983–1006.

Tarski, A. (1956) *Logic, Semantics, Metamathematics*, Oxford, UK: Clarendon Press.

Taylor, C. (1986) "Foucault on Freedom and Truth", in D. Hoy (ed.) *Foucault: A Critical Reader*, Oxford, UK; New York: Basil Blackwell.

Turner, M. (1996) *The Literary Mind*, Oxford, UK; New York: Oxford University Press.

Vlastos, G. (1991) *Socrates: Ironist and Moral Philosopher*, Ithaca, NY: Cornell University Press.

Weber, S. (1977) "The Divaricator: Remarks on Freud's *Witz*," *Glyph*, 1.

Weintraub, R. (1989) "Methodology Doesn't Matter, But the History of Thought Might," *Scandinavian Journal of Economics*, 91, 2, 477–93.

—— (1999) "How Should We Write the History of Twentieth-Century Economics?" *Oxford Review of Economic Policy*, 15, 4, 139–52.

Wilber, C. and Harrison, R. (1978) "The Methodological Basis of Institutional Economics: Pattern Model, Storytelling, and Holism," *Journal of Economic Issues*, 12.

Wilber, C. and Hoksbergen, R. (1986) "Ethical Values and Economic Theory: A Survey," *Religious Studies Review*, 12, 3/4, 205–14.

Wilson, E. O. (1975) *Sociobiology: The New Synthesis*, Cambridge, MA: Harvard University Press.

—— (1978) *On Human Nature*, Cambridge, MA: Harvard University Press.

—— (1998) *Consilience: The Unity of Knowledge*, New York: Random House (Vintage Books).

Ziman, J. (1994) *Prometheus Bound*, Cambridge, UK; New York: Cambridge University Press.

Index